LETTING THE GOOD ONES GO

A Leader's Guide to Approaching Layoffs with Care and Compassion

LETTING THE GOOD ONES GO

A Leader's Guide to Approaching Layoffs with Care and Compassion

By Dan H. Lawrence

BRICKALOW
Publishing House

Denver, Colorado

Published by Brickalow Publishing House
Denver, Colorado

For inquiries, contact Brickalow Publishing House at: brickalow@gmail.com.

Library of Congress Control Number: 2025934707

ISBN (paperback): 979-8-9924153-2-2

ISBN (epub): 979-8-9924153-3-9

Table of Contents

Introduction

---

*"To handle yourself, use your head; to
handle others, use your heart."*
— Eleanor Roosevelt

I didn't set out to write a book about layoffs. However, when I became the face of budget cuts in a mission-driven organization, I had to learn what it meant to lead with integrity, especially when the decisions were painful.

Learning the Hard Way

When I first stepped into my role as Dean in a private university, I made mistakes. Not just small ones, but missteps that had real consequences for people who had already endured years of cuts, uncertainty, and frustration. I walked into a unit that had been systematically downsized over time, where staff had repeatedly adapted to doing more with less until there was barely anything left to give.

At the time of my arrival, the institution was taking steps to align its budget with long-term shifts in enrollment and revenue. On paper, it was the right call. But for the people affected, those who had spent years watching their resources dwindle, it was yet another blow. They had spent years tightening belts, cutting corners, and making sacrifices, only to be met with another administrator telling them that more had to go.

That administrator was *me*. I became the face of yet another round of budget cuts.

I didn't fully grasp what I had walked into. My decisions were quick, pragmatic, and made with the best intentions of financial stewardship. But I didn't fully understand the human impact, not really. I had the privilege of knowing my own job was secure. But for those facing cuts, I was just another leader perpetuating the same cycle of loss.

I soon realized that I had to learn, quickly, how to lead differently. I had to shift my mindset from that of an administrator balancing a budget to one who could be a better servant leader, committed to a trauma-informed approach. I needed to shift my focus from making the "right" financial decision to making ethical, compassionate decisions in an inherently complex situation.

Not even two years into my job, I faced my third set of budget cuts and my second round of layoffs. I had learned from my mistakes, and I was committed to doing better. While that knowledge didn't make the process easier, I knew I could leverage what I had learned to improve the experience for the people impacted, for the staff who remained, and for me as a leader trying to do right in an impossible situation.

This book is the result of that transformation. It's not about justifying layoffs or making them palatable. It's about ensuring that, when these decisions must be made, they are done with care, with dignity, and with an understanding of the real impact they have on people's lives. It's about giving leaders the tools to handle the worst parts of their jobs in the best possible way so they can walk away knowing they did right by the people they had to let go.

I'm not writing this as an expert. I'm writing this as a decision-maker who has had to make some of the toughest decisions of my career, made mistakes along the way, and learned to do better. If you're reading this, you're likely in a situation where your choices will have an impact on people you care about. My goal is to provide a framework that helps you navigate these decisions with confidence. Then, when you do look back, you can say, *"I did what had to be done, but I did it with care and compassion."*

A Relational Misstep in a Relational Organization

When I stepped into this role, I had no intention of making any major changes for at least six months, or possibly a year, if things ran smoothly. My plan was simple: get to know my staff, build relationships, and understand the people I was leading, not just their job functions but what they loved about their work. I wanted to get a sense of what was working, what wasn't, and what mattered most to the people in my unit. I wanted to hear their stories, learn about the challenges they faced, and position myself as a partner in their mission. I didn't want to be just another administrator with a different vision.

And I did listen. At first.

In my initial conversations, faculty and staff shared with me their experiences of years of budget cuts and incremental losses that had eroded their ability to do their work. But what stood out, and came up again and again, was the absence of professional development funding.

They had been without it for years. No conference travel. No external training. No resources to stay current in their fields. They weren't just missing opportunities for career growth; they were missing connections to the broader professional world.

For ranked faculty, especially, this wasn't just about travel or training. It was about feeling valued. About being seen as professionals. About being part of something beyond the institution's walls.

So, despite the financial realities, I made it a priority to restore professional development funds. It was an early win, a signal to my team that I had heard them, that I understood what mattered to them. And it was appreciated. But then the cuts came.

Well, That Was a Mistake

About a month into my new role, before I even finished settling in, I received my first round of bad news: a mid-fiscal-year budget reduction was coming. Instead of spending time with my team, learning from them, and getting a clear understanding of the unit's culture, I shifted my focus into problem-solving mode.

I told myself that the best way I could serve my team was to secure resources, fight for funding, and keep us as intact as possible.

I saw my primary role as positioning my unit within the larger institution, building and rebuilding relationships across campus, and ensuring we were seen as valuable in an increasingly competitive budget environment. I had to advocate, strategize, and align with institutional priorities. My job wasn't just to protect us in the short term but to ensure we had a voice at the table in the long term.

So I focused externally.

I protected my unit and positioned us well in the larger institution. Our budget reductions were smaller than in some areas, even if only by single-digit percentages. I started repairing relationships with other units and building new ones. In the end, I was even able to reallocate some unexpected savings into modest salary increases to address some longstanding pay disparities that my department heads had alerted me to as a source of poor morale during my first weeks on the job.

But the more I focused outward, the less present I was internally. I spent less time focusing on the relationships I needed to build inside my own unit, and that was a big mistake in an organization as deeply relational as ours.

Trust isn't something you earn once and then move on. It's built over time, through relationships, through showing up not just when advocating for resources, but in the day-to-day moments that shape an organization's culture.

Without these strong internal relationships, I remained an outsider in their eyes, a representative of institutional decisions rather than a trusted partner in their work.

I Became Just Another Administrator

The first round of cuts had been painful but manageable. The choice between cutting "people or stuff" was clear, and I chose to protect jobs. We tightened budgets, eliminated discretionary spending, and found creative ways to stretch resources. I reassured myself and my team that we were doing everything possible to avoid directly impacting people.

For a while, it worked. But when deeper reductions were announced months later, everything changed.

I wanted to handle the situation with care, but I was at a disadvantage. I was the first dean hired from outside the unit in decades. Unlike my department heads and long-serving staff, I hadn't spent years in the trenches with them. I hadn't been there for the past rounds of cuts. I wasn't someone who had fought alongside them. I didn't have that history. I hadn't earned their trust. To them, I became yet another administrator in a long line of administrators delivering more bad news.

It didn't matter that I was advocating behind the scenes to minimize the impact. It didn't matter that I was agonizing over every decision. All they saw and felt was the impact.

And it wasn't just financial, it was deeply personal.

For years, they had been told to do more with less. They had absorbed loss after loss, each one adding weight to their workload and emotional strain. They had watched their teams shrink, their responsibilities grow, and their ability to serve students, faculty, and the broader community slowly erode.

And now, as they saw it, here I was asking them to absorb even more.

The resentment wasn't just about the need for layoffs; it was about the cumulative exhaustion of never feeling secure, never feeling heard, and never feeling like they had control over their own futures. And I hadn't done enough to help them see me as anything other than another decision-maker at a distance.

This was just as frustrating for me as it was for them. I had a plan, a long-term vision. I was doing this for them, the unit, and the institution. I was on my way to securing grant funding to generate revenue, foster relationships, and enhance our visibility. All they could see was me asking them to do more, for me, for something I wanted. They didn't trust me or my purpose.

That lack of trust made everything harder for me and for them. Because without a foundation of trust, even the best-intentioned decisions feel like betrayals.

The Unintended Consequences of Doing Less with Less

I believed that by cutting operational costs first, I was making the least harmful choice. Cut the stuff, keep the people. It was a simple equation. But I failed to account for the hidden cost.

The impact of those cuts wasn't just financial, it was emotional.

Every dollar saved meant a program that no longer had resources. A service that was harder to provide. A problem that took longer to solve. For my staff, it wasn't just about making numbers work. It was about the students, faculty, and community members they served.

They weren't just employees, they were caretakers. Every reduction, even when it didn't directly impact their jobs, felt like another blow to the work they cared about. And when I stood before them, explaining the rationale, I realized that logic and understanding weren't enough.

Then came the second round of cuts. This time, there was nothing left to trim. The choice wasn't between people or stuff anymore. It was people or people. We left vacant positions unfilled. We restructured workloads. And for the first time, someone had to be told their job would be eliminated.

And while my staff understood, having seen the writing on the wall and knowing cuts were inevitable, that didn't make it any easier. Because every empty desk wasn't just a position lost, it was another gap in services. It was another student who wouldn't get the same level of guidance. It was another faculty member who would have to wait longer for help. It was another program that had once been thriving but would now barely be holding on.

That's when the frustration turned into something deeper: mourning.

They mourned the work they could no longer do and the support they could no longer provide. The sense of mission that had once driven them was now overshadowed by exhaustion and uncertainty. They had spent years picking up the slack after every cut, doing everything in their power to keep things afloat, but there was no slack left to pick up.

I had hoped that shifting our mindset from *"do more with less"* to *"do less with less"* would help ease the pressure. By openly acknowledging that we couldn't continue stretching beyond our limits, I could give my staff permission to let go of certain responsibilities.

But for them, *letting go* wasn't that simple.

People in caring professions don't just stop caring about the people they serve because the budget says so. They don't turn off the part of themselves that wants to help. When leadership says, *"We have to do less,"* what employees often hear is:

"We have to stop doing things that matter."

That's when mourning turns into anger.

And this is where it all compounded. They understood the reality of the cuts. They didn't think I could magically make money appear. But every decision, every reduction, every position left vacant, and every service scaled back felt like a *choice* to let someone down. And those choices added up. No matter how carefully I explained the reasoning or tried to convince them (and myself) that we would overcome this setback, it didn't change the outcome.

I had underestimated how much that weight would break them.

Budget cuts don't just shape an institution's bottom line; they shape its culture, its trust, and its future. Repeated budget cuts, especially when they result in layoffs, leave a lasting imprint, not just on the people who lose their jobs but on those who stay, forced to navigate what's left.

Because leadership isn't just about survival. It's about sustaining the people who make survival possible.

If I wanted my team to keep showing up, I had to show them that leadership isn't just about making the hard calls. It's about making them in a way that acknowledges the weight of those difficult decisions.

Why This Book Exists

I never thought I'd write a book about letting people go.

Like many in leadership roles across education, healthcare, public service, and nonprofit work, I didn't step into this career expecting to deliver layoff notices. I chose a path rooted in care where people work long hours for modest pay because they believe in something bigger than themselves. In my case, that belief was in the power of education to transform lives and communities.

But even in caring professions, we end up in impossible situations. One day, you're advocating for student success or fighting for community impact. The next, you're sitting across from a colleague who's given years to the mission, and telling them their job is ending. It feels like a betrayal. Not just of that person, but of the values that brought you here in the first place.

I began writing this book during my time as a first-time dean at a private university in the Western U.S. It was a higher education institution grappling with the same long-term enrollment declines and budget challenges facing so many others. I came in with plans for thoughtful, strategic refinement. I was relatively confident that strategic planning, careful budgeting, and efficiency would keep us on steady ground. But what I hadn't fully grasped was the weight of cumulative loss. Year after year of shrinking budgets, deferred maintenance, and exhausted staff stretched beyond their limits.

I had stepped into this role with the hope of making thoughtful, strategic refinements with the precision of a scalpel, ensuring we could maintain our core mission while minimizing harm. But the reality was far more challenging. At times, I had to make broad, sweeping reductions that felt more like clearing a path through tangled, overgrown terrain with a machete. Removing not just excess but things of value as well. It didn't take long before I realized that the choices before us were no longer about streamlining; they were about survival.

And I was the one who had to make these difficult, imperfect, often heartbreaking choices.

Over time, I realized this wasn't just about financial strategy. Behind every spreadsheet entry was a person with relationships, history, and purpose tied to their work. Each decision carried emotional weight. And how I made those decisions mattered just as much as what I decided.

I wrote this book because, too often, leaders in caring professions like education, healthcare, and nonprofits are given little guidance on how to make tough choices in a way that preserves dignity, trust, and humanity. We are expected to navigate these moments with professionalism, but what does that actually mean? How do we communicate layoffs with honesty and care? How do we support those who leave while also tending to the employees who remain? And, perhaps hardest of all, how do we carry the weight of these decisions ourselves without becoming numb to the human cost?

This book is not a leadership manifesto or a how-to guide for corporate downsizing. Instead, it reflects on what it means to lead with integrity in the most challenging moments and serves as a guide for those who must make the tough decisions they never wanted to make.

Who This Book Is For

This book is geared toward leaders in organizations serving the public good, whose careers are driven by a mission to serve others. For those who have ever stayed late at work, not because you were chasing wealth, but chasing purpose... because it mattered to the well-being of others. For those who have chosen impact over income, even when the bills were tight. If you've ever poured yourself into a job because you believed it made a difference, then this book is for you.

I know you didn't take your job with the intention to make decisions about who stays and who goes. But now, you're here. And you're faced with a choice: do this the easy way, or do this with care and compassion?

Does that mean that others can't benefit from this approach? Of course not. Corporate executives relying on managers shuffling numbers on a spreadsheet to cut nameless positions and boost profits could learn a thing or two as well. We could all use a little more compassion.

What This Book Covers

I'm not an HR expert. This isn't a manual on legal compliance, severance packages, or restructuring strategy. This leadership book is about making hard decisions and letting people go in a way that allows you to sleep at night. This book addresses:

- ❖ How to prepare for layoffs with transparency and fairness
- ❖ How to deliver the news in a way that preserves dignity

- ❖ How to support departing employees
- ❖ How to lead the remaining team through survivor's guilt and instability
- ❖ How to take care of yourself as a leader navigating these decisions

If you're reading this, you're likely in a position no one wants to be in. Maybe you're weeks away from making tough calls. Maybe you've already had to let people go and are grappling with the aftermath.

My goal is simple: to help you lead with integrity, act with compassion, and make sure that, when the dust settles, you know you did everything you could to honor the people affected.

I won't lie to you. This work is brutal. But it doesn't have to be heartless.

Before you move forward, take a moment to reflect, not on the logistics of budget cuts or the mechanics of layoffs, but on what leadership means to you in general, especially in moments of crisis.

- ❖ **Your Leadership Values**: When you first stepped into leadership, what did you believe was most important? Have the challenges you've faced reaffirmed those values or tested them?
- ❖ **The Weight of Responsibility**: Think back to the hardest decision you've had to make. Was it about numbers, or was it about people? How did you handle it? How did it change you?
- ❖ **Trust and Relationships**: Leadership isn't just about making hard decisions; it's about how those

decisions are experienced by the people you lead. Who trusts you right now? Who doesn't? What would it take to repair or strengthen those relationships?

Take a breath. Acknowledge the weight of this work. And remember, leadership isn't just about the choices you make, it's about how you make them.

Chapter 1
The New Reality of Mission-Driven Sector Budget Cuts

"The lesson of history is that you do not get a sustained economic recovery as long as the financial system is in crisis."
– Ben Bernanke

Mission-driven, or "caring," organizations serving the public good—whether in education, social services, public agencies, or nonprofits—are facing a reckoning. The financial models that have sustained us for decades are breaking down, and for many of us in leadership, this moment feels different.

For years, when money got tight, we did what we always do: tightened budgets, increased fundraising efforts, found creative ways to stretch every dollar, and held onto the belief that, eventually, things would stabilize. However, we're now starting to see the bigger picture, and this isn't just another downturn. It's not a temporary budget crunch. We're living through a fundamental shift in how socially responsible work is funded, prioritized, and valued.

For me, this realization didn't come all at once. It came in pieces, through endless budget spreadsheets where the numbers didn't add up, through difficult conversations with staff and faculty who had been through too many rounds of cuts, and through the growing awareness that no amount of efficiency could fix what was happening. We weren't just being asked to tighten our belts. We were being asked to rethink everything.

And what's making it worse? The chaos at the federal level with cuts to programs, mass layoffs, and the on-again, off-again funding freezes, means that the institutions and organizations people rely on most are being squeezed from every direction.

I've spent my career in higher education, state agencies, and the nonprofit sector, and I know this isn't just about one industry. Nonprofits, government agencies, libraries, research institutions, and social service organizations are all weathering the same storm. Financial instability, shifting priorities, and funding uncertainties are hitting every mission-driven sector simultaneously. The truth is, many of us are navigating uncharted waters, trying to find a way forward when the old maps no longer apply.

The Federal Funding Crisis: A Domino Effect on Mission-Driven Work

In early 2025, an event occurred that sent shockwaves through sectors like mine. The federal government began freezing thousands of programs and grants. The official reason? A "funding reassessment." The real-world impact? Organizations that depended on those funds suddenly found themselves in limbo, unable to pay staff, fund services, or continue critical research projects.

I watched as nonprofits, public institutions, and even state agencies scrambled to make sense of it. Programs supporting everything from education to medical services, research to public aid, stalled overnight. The uncertainty alone caused damage. Leaders couldn't plan, staff couldn't be paid, and services that people relied on were suddenly at risk.

And then, just as organizations started to regain footing, a second blow hit: an unprecedented push to downsize the federal workforce by 75% as part of a sweeping budget-cutting initiative.

Think about that for a moment. That's not just cutting some red tape. That's eliminating entire departments, gutting federal agencies, and destabilizing the very systems that provide funding and infrastructure for education, healthcare, research, and public welfare.

As of the time this book was written, legal battles over funding cuts, layoffs, and policy shifts are still being played out in the courts, but the damage began long before any rulings were handed down. The sheer volume of announcements, Dear Colleague Letters, and restructuring plans sent a shockwave through mission-driven sectors, creating an immediate ripple effect.

Even before the courts could weigh in, organizations began bracing for impact. This anticipatory compliance, the instinct to prepare for the worst before it was even required, led institutions to freeze hiring, pause programs, and preemptively cut budgets and important programs. Websites were updated or removed, grant-funded initiatives were shelved, research projects were put on hold, and agencies that rely on federal dollars began scaling back services. Not because of directives, but because the uncertainty made it too risky to move forward as planned.

For many organizations, it wasn't just about following the letter of the law, it was about survival. When funding will be restored, guidelines keep shifting, and every headline hints at another potential disruption, the safest move is often to pull back. The chilling effect took hold quickly, as colleges, nonprofits, and government agencies tried to stay ahead of changes that had yet to be finalized.

And the consequences? Fewer resources were available for those who needed them most. Staff were suspended in doubt, unsure if their jobs would still exist in the coming week. Communities were losing critical services not because of an official policy decision but because organizations were making conservative choices in the face of overwhelming uncertainty.

Even if some of these federal cuts or restrictions are later overturned, the damage is already done. Anticipatory compliance has already reshaped budgets, staffing decisions, and institutional priorities, which are unlikely to be restored once cut.

Feeling the Impact

For colleges and universities, the financial struggles were already there. Declining enrollment, skyrocketing costs, and a growing skepticism about the value of a degree meant that institutions were already operating on thin margins. However, with the sudden uncertainty in federal funding, things worsened.

Research universities that relied on grants to fund scientific and medical advancements suddenly had projects put on hold or halted altogether. Public institutions, already seeing reduced state funding, found themselves having to make even deeper cuts. And private colleges, many of which had been discounting tuition just to stay competitive, were running out of ways to balance the books.

I saw firsthand how this played out in my own institution. We were put at risk of losing access to grant funding. Revenue from international students began to vanish as visa approvals slowed, stalled, or stopped altogether, caught in the uncertainty of changing federal rules and backlogs. Students who rely on federal aid to stay enrolled, many of whom are first-generation or low-income, are now wondering if that support will still be available in the following semester.

And it wasn't just higher education that was experiencing this uncertainty. The nonprofit world was experiencing the same thing. Social services that depended on government contracts saw funding pulled. Aid organizations that had built their budgets around promised federal dollars were now struggling to survive. Libraries, state agencies, public research institutes, and community outreach programs all found themselves on shaky ground.

What made this moment different was that there was nowhere to turn for relief. Historically, when one revenue source shrank, another might step in, such as grants, philanthropy, or public-private partnerships. But this time, everything was tightening at once.

This Isn't Just a Budget Crisis, It's a Systemic Shift

For a while, I kept telling myself (and my staff) that this was just another tough cycle. That if we could just get through this year, things would stabilize. However, the more I examined the numbers, the more I realized we weren't dealing with a short-term crisis. We were watching the system during a transformation.

I kept going back to the same question: What happens when there's nothing left to cut?

The truth is, many of us have already been cutting budgets for years. My institution had been experiencing death by a thousand paper cuts. Small budget reductions, hiring freezes, and program consolidations, all to stretch limited dollars just a little further.

And now? Now, we were being asked to go beyond trimming the fat. We were being asked to fundamentally rethink what we do and how we do it.

This wasn't about efficiency anymore. It was about survival.

What This Means for Leadership

The most dangerous thing we can do right now is pretend that this is just another cycle. That if we just wait it out, things will return to the way they were. That kind of thinking leads to short-term fixes when what we need are long-term strategies.

The reality is that we are not just managing temporary budget reductions; we are leading through a systemic transformation. Institutions, agencies, and organizations that fail to recognize this will continue to make cuts around the edges, hoping for a turnaround that isn't forthcoming.

Instead, we have to ask harder questions:

❖ What does sustainability look like in this new landscape?
❖ How do we serve our missions with fewer resources, permanently?
❖ What do we let go of? Not just temporarily, but for good?

These are the kinds of questions that many of us hoped we'd never have to ask. But avoiding them doesn't change the reality we're facing. And if we don't acknowledge what's really happening, we risk making decisions that only delay the inevitable rather than preparing our institutions for what's next. For many of us, the next step is unavoidable, but no less painful.

We have to cut people.

And that's the part no one wants to talk about.

Budget models can be adjusted, expenses trimmed, and programs consolidated, but at some point, the numbers don't work unless payroll shrinks. The reality is stark: institutions aren't just tightening belts anymore, they're fundamentally reshaping what they can afford to be.

And with every decision to eliminate a position, we're not just reducing costs. We're impacting real lives.

When it comes to layoffs, leadership must move beyond its narrow financial strategy blinders and accept the importance of elevating values. How we handle these moments, how we communicate them, how we support people through them, and how we carry the weight of these decisions, will define not just our institutions but our integrity as leaders.

Values in Crisis: Leadership in Difficult Times

When budgets tighten, it's easy to think of financial cuts as a math problem or to reduce everything down to spreadsheets and revenue streams. But that's not leadership.

Leadership is making difficult decisions that impact real people while staying true to the values that define us.

As I faced my first round of staff reductions, I had to ask myself:

"What kind of leader do I want to be when things get hard? What values guide my decision-making? How do I balance financial reality with human dignity?"

As my institution faced more serious reductions to the workforce, I learned that leadership in crisis means:

- ❖ **Transparency**: Telling people the truth, even when it's uncomfortable.

❖ **Dignity:** Recognizing that job loss is deeply personal and needs to be treated with respect.
❖ **Compassion**: Understanding that these changes have real emotional consequences.
❖ **Fairness**: Ensuring that the process is thoughtful and not arbitrary.
❖ **Responsibility**: Acknowledging my role in guiding the organization through uncertainty.

These aren't just abstract ideas. They offer practical leadership perspectives that shape how we approach difficult choices.

If we don't lead with values, we reduce people to numbers. When people feel like they've been treated as expendable, we lose not just employees but also trust, morale, and the integrity of our institutions.

Why Leading with Values Matters

Here's the reality: Budget cuts will happen. People will lose their jobs. The financial constraints aren't going away. But how we handle these moments is what defines us as leaders and as institutions.

The choice is simple:

- We can cut without care. We can rip off the Band-Aid, prioritize speed over people, and create an organization that runs on fear.
- Or we can lay off with care and compassion, recognizing that while we can't control economic realities, we can control how people experience them.

One of these approaches destroys morale and trust. The other, while still painful, allows people to walk away with respect, clarity, and understanding.

And that difference? That's the true work of leadership.

Chapter 1 Summary

In this chapter, we examined the financial crisis affecting mission-driven organizations. This isn't just another budget shortfall or economic downturn; it's a systemic shift in how socially responsible work is funded, prioritized, and valued.

The instability created by federal funding freezes, mass layoffs, and shifting economic priorities has left institutions scrambling. Anticipatory compliance has led many organizations to preemptively cut programs, reduce staffing, and scale back services, not because they were required to do so, but because uncertainty made long-term planning impossible.

For many institutions, this moment is the breaking point after years of financial strain. The era of "trimming the fat" is over. What's left are fundamental decisions about what organizations can afford to be. We are making the decisions that will define leadership, institutional integrity, and the futures of the people affected.

In the next chapter, we'll move from financial realities to the human side of layoffs. We'll discuss how job cuts affect individuals, teams, and institutional culture, and how leaders can approach them with care and integrity.

Chapter 1 Takeaways

❖ **We're in a Systemic Shift, not a Temporary Budget Crunch.** Mission-driven organizations are facing a long-term financial transformation, not just a short-term crisis. The old funding models are no longer sustainable.

❖ **The Ripple Effect of Federal Cuts is Immediate and Widespread.** Government funding freezes and federal layoffs aren't just impacting direct employees; they destabilize entire ecosystems of education, research, social services, and nonprofit work.

❖ **Anticipatory Compliance has Already Reshaped Organizations.** Even before formal policies take effect, institutions are bracing for impact by freezing hiring, shelving grant-funded projects, and restructuring services; sometimes making cuts before they're necessary.

❖ **There's Nothing Left to Trim, Only Difficult Choices to Make.** Many institutions have already endured years of budget reductions, hiring freezes, and program cuts. Now, survival means making fundamental decisions about what to prioritize, rather than seeking small efficiencies.

❖ **Leadership in Crisis Requires Values-Driven Decisions.** Cutting budgets isn't just about financial strategy; it's about people. How leaders handle these decisions will define institutional culture, morale, and trust for years to come.

Reflection: Facing Financial Realities as a Leader

- ❖ What financial assumptions have shaped my leadership decisions? Have they changed in light of current realities?
- ❖ What past budget strategies (e.g., small cuts, hiring freezes) are no longer effective? What alternatives need to be considered?
- ❖ How have financial constraints affected the morale and effectiveness of my team?
- ❖ What does sustainability look like in my organization now? What difficult choices will need to be made?

Chapter 2
The Human Cost of Downsizing

"People want to know they matter, and they want to be treated as people. That's the new talent contract." – Pamela Stroko

---

No graduate program prepared me for this. No leadership training truly conveyed what it feels like to sit across from someone who has poured years into their work, someone who has built relationships, someone who has done nothing wrong, and tell them their job is gone.

There are books about financial planning, restructuring strategies, and crisis communication. HR has bullet points for compliance, severance, and benefits. But none of that prepares you for the moment you look someone in the eye and deliver news that upends their life.

Layoffs are often framed as a financial necessity, a numbers game, a strategic restructuring. But for the people affected, it's deeply personal. Losing a job is not just about income; it's about identity, stability, and dignity. It's about the people they served and the work they believed in. It's about their plans for their future, the bills they still have to pay, the children they have to support, the home they hope to keep.

And for those of us delivering the news, it's about holding the weight of those losses while trying to convince ourselves that we're making the best decision in an impossible situation.

This chapter isn't about budget strategies or legal compliance. It's about what often gets overlooked, the psychological and emotional toll of layoffs, not just on individuals, but on entire organizations. Too often, leadership focuses on logistics like what positions to cut, how to restructure, how to "minimize disruption" without fully acknowledging the human impact.

Layoffs don't happen in isolation. Their effects ripple through workplace culture, reshaping trust, morale, and stability. If unaddressed, these changes don't just harm individuals. They undermine the very institution we're trying to protect. A layoff isn't just a financial event; it's an organizational crisis.

Leaders who miss this reality create emotionally unsafe workplaces where trust erodes, morale collapses, and employees brace for the next blow. Those who leave grieve, but so do those who stay. A workforce in constant fear cannot fully engage.

And that's where so many organizations get it wrong.

We focus on logistics—the savings, the restructuring—but underestimate the emotional cost. We assume people will simply move on. But job loss isn't just a transaction; it's a profound disruption that carries real emotional weight.

The question isn't whether layoffs will impact people, they will. The real question is how leadership will respond.

Ignoring the human cost creates lasting damage: broken trust, disengagement, and resentment that lingers long after the financial crisis ends. This chapter isn't about the financial consequences of emotional fallout. It's about our responsibility to each other.

Leadership isn't just about making hard decisions, it's about how we make them, how we communicate them, and how we help people move through them. True leadership recognizes that job loss is a personal crisis that shakes identity, stability, and trust. The ripple effects extend far beyond the individuals affected, creating workplace trauma that, if left unhealed, weakens the entire organization.

Leading through layoffs with care ensures that an organization doesn't just survive, it remains a place where people can still believe in its mission.

The Grief of Job Loss: Understanding the Emotional Toll

We don't often talk about job loss in the same way we talk about other major life losses like divorce, the death of a loved one, or a serious health crisis. But the emotional experience is strikingly similar.

Work provides more than just a paycheck. It gives people a sense of purpose, structure, and belonging. It's a place where friendships are formed, skills are developed, and people feel like they matter. Losing that and being told, *"We no longer have a place for you,"* disrupts all of this.

For those who experience layoffs firsthand, there is an immediate and jarring loss of stability. Beyond financial concerns, there's the psychological weight of feeling unwanted or disposable. Even when employees experiencing a layoff logically understand that the decision wasn't personal, it still feels personal. They question their worth, their skills, and their future.

For those who remain, the experience is far from easy. Layoffs fracture workplace relationships, shake confidence in leadership, and create an undercurrent of anxiety. Those left behind often feel guilty about still having their jobs, resentful of the additional workload, tenuous about their own job security, or simply unsure if their loyalty to the organization is still warranted.

Psychologists often compare job loss to the five stages of grief. These stages don't always happen in order, and people may cycle through them multiple times. But recognizing them can help us understand why layoffs hit so hard, and why they don't just affect those who lose their jobs.

Denial: The Refusal to Accept What's Happening

First, there's disbelief. "This can't really be happening. Surely, there's been a mistake. Maybe the funding will come through. Maybe leadership will reconsider." Employees facing layoffs often cling to any hope that the decision might be reversed, that something, anything, will change to make it all go away.

But denial doesn't just affect those who lose their jobs It ripples through the entire organization. Those who remain convince themselves that things will return to normal soon, that this is just another rough patch. Leadership, too, hopes that if they can just push through, stability will return.

I know this because I did it myself.

After my first round of budget cuts, I told myself this was just a tough year, an adjustment. Following the second round of cuts, I began scrutinizing the projections more closely, but I still believed we could make it through with careful planning. As we embarked on the third round of budget cuts, I saw what I couldn't admit before: more often than not, these moments aren't temporary setbacks, they're turning points.

I remember sitting in my office after a difficult budget announcement, staring at the numbers, trying to convince myself that we'd find another solution. I grasped for any reassurance that we wouldn't have to make the hard decisions, that something would change if we just held on long enough.

It was only later, too much later, that I realized how much time I had wasted in denial. Time I could have spent preparing my staff to make the transition smoother and helping people process what was coming, rather than leaving them in the dark.

Denial is a natural defense mechanism, a way to soften the emotional blow. But as a leader, I've learned that failing to communicate openly and honestly only allows false hope to linger. And when false hope lingers, it prevents people from processing the loss and preparing for what comes next.

The hardest part of moving past denial is admitting that stability isn't always just around the corner. Sometimes, things don't go back to normal. Sometimes, normal doesn't exist anymore. And that's when leadership has to step up, not by offering false reassurances, but by helping people navigate what's real, even when reality is painful.

Anger: The Search for Someone to Blame

When the reality sets in, frustration follows. Why me? Why wasn't someone else let go? After all the extra hours, the dedication, the sacrifices, how could this happen to me?

Those who remain feel it, too, but their anger is often directed elsewhere. Why them and not me? Who made this decision? Could leadership have handled the situation differently?

And then, there's the anger no one talks about, the leader's anger. The frustration of being forced into impossible decisions. The resentment of being the one delivering the news, knowing that you didn't cause this crisis but are left to clean up the consequences. The helplessness of knowing that no matter how carefully you made the cuts, people will still see you as the villain.

Anger is one of the most volatile stages of grief. It can lead to workplace tension, outbursts, or a breakdown of trust. Some employees lash out on social media, some inappropriately vent to their students, while others withdraw, becoming disengaged, resentful, or openly hostile.

Anger can be deeply uncomfortable for leaders, especially those who deliver the news. The instinct is to explain, to justify, to point to financial constraints or efficiency measures. But logical reasoning rarely soothes an emotional wound.

Anger isn't a problem to be solved; it's a response to loss. And the worst thing a leader can do is dismiss it, whether it's the anger of their employees or their own.

If anger is ignored, it doesn't fade; it festers. It turns into bitterness, distrust, and disengagement that linger long after the layoffs happen. People need space to vent and ask why, even if they already know the answer. They need to say out loud that it isn't fair because it isn't.

When the second round of budget cuts was announced, there was a lot of frustration that ultimately focused on my leadership. I held a public listening session, hoping to hear ideas, solutions, collaborations, and ways we might move forward together. But that is not what happened. Instead, faculty and staff used the space to voice their frustrations. It wasn't easy to sit through. The work I had done on the salary adjustments and the restored professional development funds felt dismissed. I became the target.

I remember thinking, *"Why don't they see what I've tried to do?"* At the time, I left that meeting feeling misunderstood, attacked, and deeply discouraged. Looking back, I see it differently. They didn't need solutions at that moment. They needed space to grieve, vent, and be heard. And I had not fully understood just how raw things still were.

The truth is that leaders need space, too. I didn't realize how much my own frustration was shaping my responses. I wanted to be fair. I wanted people to understand that I was not making these decisions lightly. When the backlash came, and people questioned my judgment, resentment started to build, and I felt defensive.

I wanted to say, *"You think I don't hate this? Do you think I don't feel sick about these choices?"* But that wasn't what they needed. They needed someone who could hold space for their pain, not try to explain it away. They needed someone who could stay grounded, even when it hurt.

This is where transparency matters. When people understand how and why decisions were made, not just in vague terms, but in real, tangible ways, it doesn't erase their anger but stops it from hardening into lasting resentment. The institutions that handle layoffs the worst are those that pretend it's nothing personal, refusing to acknowledge the weight of what's happening. But when leadership makes space for people to process their frustration, ask hard questions, and get real answers, the path forward, however painful, becomes clearer.

Bargaining: The Search for an Alternative

When faced with job loss, people seek ways to regain control when they feel they have none. *"What if I take a pay cut? What if I move to part-time? Could I switch departments?"* They grasp at any possibility that might change the outcome, hoping to make themselves indispensable.

And it's not just those who are being laid off. Those who remain engage in their own form of bargaining, convincing themselves that if they work harder, take on extra responsibilities, or prove their value, they'll be safe. *"If I stay late every night, if I volunteer for every project, if I show them how much they need me, maybe I won't be next."*

This is how toxic overwork cultures take root. Employees push themselves beyond their limits, believing their survival depends on it. However, the hard truth is that no amount of extra effort can prevent a layoff when the decision is driven by budget constraints. And when that realization sets in, when someone has given everything they have and still finds themselves at risk, the grief deepens.

I've watched people throw themselves into their work, desperately trying to outrun uncertainty. I've done it myself, believing that if I just worked harder, built the right connections, and stayed ahead of the next financial crisis, I could shield myself from whatever came next. But layoffs don't work that way. They aren't always about individual performance. And when people tie their self-worth to their job security, they set themselves up for exhaustion, resentment, and burnout.

This kind of bargaining often occurs during restructuring, which frequently accompanies downsizing. It's less about the proposed change and more about the disruption to what people have known: the status quo that offered stability, predictability, and a sense of control.

In one case, during the most recent round of budget cuts, the voluntary departure of a department head opened the door for a merger that promised substantial cost savings. It was a clear financial win and an option to be seriously considered. In another instance, a proposed consolidation offered only modest savings but brought long-term strategic and operational benefits. Still, in both cases, I found myself in conversations with managers who urged me to wait; to hold off on the change until it was "absolutely necessary."

In many ways, they were really asking to preserve what felt familiar. The resistance wasn't always about the numbers. It was about the emotional cost of change, about grieving a structure they had invested in and understood. In these moments, bargaining became a way to resist the discomfort of uncertainty and delay the loss of what had once felt like solid ground.

Bargaining creates false hope, and when leaders fail to address it directly, it can lead to long-term damage. Employees mourn the loss of their colleagues, but they also mourn the loss of stability, predictability, and the belief that effort and loyalty will keep them safe. When that belief is shattered, so is trust.

Depression: When Reality Sets In

At some point, the initial shock fades, the anger quiets, and what's left is the heavy, lingering weight of loss.

For those who have lost their jobs, the uncertainty of what comes next can be paralyzing. Even the most skilled, dedicated employees start to doubt themselves. *"What if I don't find another job? What if I can't support my family? What if I was never as good as I thought I was?"* The professional world moves fast, and it's easy to feel like you've been left behind.

For those left behind, the workplace feels different, emptier, quieter. Desks sit vacant. Email signatures disappear. The people they collaborated with, leaned on, and shared daily conversations with are suddenly gone. Meetings that once felt energized now feel strained. The fear of another round of cuts lingers, making it hard to focus on anything beyond just getting through the day.

I've felt it, too. After my first round of cuts, I thought things would stabilize and that the worst was behind us. But then the second round came, and then, with the third round of cuts, I see how naive that hope was. The loss isn't just about numbers in a budget, it's about people I respected, people I worked alongside, people whose absence is felt in ways I never anticipated. And I know I'm not the only one feeling it.

Some employees check out emotionally. They do their work, but the sense of purpose that once fueled them is gone. Others withdraw from workplace culture, disengaging from conversations, brainstorming sessions, and the informal camaraderie that once made the job meaningful. I even felt myself withdrawing, especially after being blamed for the cuts.

And then there's the weight of survivor's guilt. *"Why was I spared when they weren't?"* A question that has no satisfying answer.

After every round of layoffs, there's a moment when the silence in the office feels heavier than the work itself. And I've learned that if I don't acknowledge it, if I pretend that things are fine when they're not, I only make it worse.

Leaders often misinterpret this phase as a sign of a lack of commitment. Productivity dips, enthusiasm wanes, and engagement falters. But it's not because employees don't care, it's because they are grieving. And grief doesn't operate on a neat timeline. The organization may have moved forward, but the people within it are still struggling to find their footing in a workplace that no longer feels the same.

Acceptance: Moving Forward, But Not Forgetting

The first time I had to lay someone off, I assumed the hardest part would be delivering the news. I thought that once the conversations were over, the organization would find its footing again, that we'd adjust, recalibrate, and move on. I didn't realize that layoffs don't just affect the people who leave; they change the people who stay.

For weeks afterward, I noticed the shift. Meetings were quieter, and people hesitated before speaking up. There was tension in the air, a collective unease as if everyone was waiting for the next shoe to drop. That's when I understood that layoffs don't end when someone packs up their desk and leaves. Their impact lingers, shaping the way people think, work, and interact long after the decisions have been made.

Eventually, people adapt. They adjust to the absence of familiar faces, to new ways of working, and to the reality that things have changed. Organizations rebuild, but they do not return to what they were before.

Layoffs leave scars. Trust in leadership erodes. People become wary, constantly bracing for the next round of cuts. Even those who weren't directly affected carry the memory of what happened, and the fear that it could happen again.

Moving forward requires more than just rebuilding budgets and restructuring teams. It requires recognizing that layoffs don't just remove positions, they change people. If we fail to address this, we're not just leading an organization through financial cuts, we're leading it into a deeper crisis.

Acceptance, in this context, doesn't mean forgetting. It means acknowledging what has happened, recognizing its impact, and making a conscious effort to rebuild, not just the organization's structure but also the trust and morale of the people who remain.

If leaders fail to acknowledge this shift, the organization risks becoming defined by unspoken grief and lingering distrust. Moving forward isn't just about filling gaps in workflows or adjusting priorities, it's about recognizing that the workplace itself has changed. And when the collective impact of these losses is ignored, it doesn't just affect morale; it reshapes the culture in ways that can be hard to undo.

The Collective Trauma of Layoffs

Even when my organization framed layoffs as "righting the ship" and finally aligning expenditures with revenue after years of overly optimistic enrollment projections, many employees didn't feel relief. They felt the weight of another loss, another restructuring, another reminder that their workplace was no longer the institution they had once known. The exhaustion was palpable, not just for those directly impacted but for everyone bracing for what might come next.

At first, I thought of it as fatigue, a natural response to ongoing change. But as people opened up, they described something deeper: they used the word trauma. It wasn't just the loss of colleagues or the added workload. It was the persistent instability, the uncertainty, the realization that no matter how well they performed, they could still be next.

I hesitated to use the word trauma at first. I didn't want to equate job loss with the generational, systemic, or life-threatening trauma many individuals and families endure. But when employees repeatedly framed their experiences that way, I had to listen. And I had to ask myself: What would it mean to lead in a way that acknowledged and responded to that collective experience?

That's when I began to understand what trauma-informed leadership truly means, a concept we'll explore in the next section. However, first, we need to examine how layoffs reshape organizational culture, not just in the short term, but in lasting and fundamental ways. Because layoffs don't just impact those who are laid off. They redefine the experience of those who stay, shaping trust in leadership, fostering a sense of security, and promoting long-term commitment to the institution.

Fear Becomes the Dominant Emotion

After layoffs are announced, a quiet but powerful shift occurs: fear takes hold. Employees become hyper-aware of their own job security. *"Am I next? If I make a mistake, will I be on the chopping block?"* They start second-guessing decisions, avoiding risk, and hesitating to take initiative. I saw this firsthand as people became noticeably more guarded around me, almost as if being noticed meant they'd be next. Conversations became shorter. Employees who once sought me out for guidance or collaboration kept their distance, and I realized it wasn't personal; it was a survival instinct.

When uncertainty lingers, self-preservation takes priority over innovation, teamwork, and creative problem-solving. The longer fear remains unaddressed, the more difficult it becomes to break the cycle.

Trust in Leadership Diminishes

Even when layoffs are unavoidable, they create a fundamental breach of trust. Employees who once felt secure in their roles now question whether leadership really has their backs. And here's the hard truth: no amount of *"We value you"* emails can undo that damage. Trust isn't rebuilt with words, it's rebuilt with actions.

This was another hard lesson learned. After our first round of university layoffs, people started leaving on their own. They had seen enough, and they no longer believed their future was safe. No matter how much I tried to reassure them that we weren't planning another round and that this was a necessary correction, they had already made up their minds. Layoffs hadn't just reduced our workforce; they had triggered an exodus of talent that I hadn't anticipated.

Productivity Drops, and Leadership Misreads It

Some leaders assume that once layoffs are over, the remaining employees will step up and "fill the gaps." However, what they often fail to recognize is that people are frequently too burned out, anxious, or grieving to function at full capacity.

A *motivation problem* occurs when employees lack the drive or incentive to perform well. They don't see a reason to put in extra effort, whether due to unclear goals, a lack of incentive, or disengagement from the work itself. A *morale problem*, on the other hand, is deeper and more serious. It's not about willingness but about emotional exhaustion, fear, and a loss of connection to the organization.

After layoffs, the real issue is almost always morale, not motivation. Employees aren't slacking because they don't care. They are overwhelmed, grieving the loss of colleagues, and uncertain about their own futures. I watched it happen firsthand: deadlines slipping, engagement dropping, teams that were once proactive now just barely hanging on. They weren't unwilling to do the work; they were simply operating in survival mode.

The real danger lies in leadership misreading the situation. When we mistake a morale problem for a motivation problem, the response tends to be more pressure, tougher expectations, motivational speeches, and demands for results. But pressure doesn't rebuild trust. What people needed in that moment wasn't to be pushed harder or to hear more reassuring platitudes. They needed stability, honesty, and space to begin healing.

Organizations that acknowledge the emotional impact of layoffs and make room for people to recover stand a much better chance of rebuilding not just productivity but loyalty and resilience for the long haul.

What Trauma-Informed Leadership Really Means

As part of my commitment to becoming a better leader, I explored what it meant to be trauma-informed. Initially rooted in social work, education, and healthcare, a trauma-informed approach recognizes the widespread impact of trauma, acknowledges how it shapes individuals and communities, and responds by fostering safety, trust, and healing. But trauma-informed leadership isn't limited to those fields; It's just as essential in organizational leadership, especially during times of crisis.

Layoffs, restructuring, and financial instability trigger stress responses similar to other forms of trauma. Employees feel powerless, uncertain, and vulnerable. Even those who aren't directly affected can experience ongoing anxiety, hypervigilance, and distrust.

Trauma-informed leaders don't just make difficult decisions; they recognize the emotional toll of those decisions and lead with empathy, transparency, and care. They understand that people aren't just reacting to a single event. They're responding to a history of uncertainty, past experiences, and the fear of what's to come.

Trauma-informed leadership doesn't mean avoiding layoffs or tough calls. It means handling them in a way that acknowledges and mitigates the harm caused.

Here are some key principles of trauma-informed leadership in times of organizational crisis:

Five Key Principles of Trauma-Informed Leadership

1. **Acknowledge the Emotional Impact: Layoffs Hurt.** Naming the loss validates employees' feelings and helps them process it. What can you do as a leader?
   - ❖ Validate emotions: "This is difficult, and it's okay to feel frustrated or upset."
   - ❖ Recognize that people will process change in different ways; some may be vocal, while others may withdraw.
   - ❖ Avoid minimizing the situation with platitudes. Be honest about the weight of the moment.

2. **Communicate with Transparency.** People don't need sugarcoating; they need clarity. Be honest about what's happening, why, and what comes next. Silence from leadership breeds distrust. Transparency, even when delivering difficult news, allows employees to process change and move forward:
   - ❖ **Before layoffs:** Don't wait until the last moment to start communicating about financial struggles.
   - ❖ **During layoffs:** Be upfront about the rationale behind decisions. Employees need to understand why and how choices were made.
   - ❖ **After layoffs:** Keep employees informed about what's next, including workload adjustments, organizational priorities, and the financial outlook.

3. **Give People Space to Grieve.** Expect sadness, frustration, and anger. Create opportunities for open conversations. Rushing people back to "business as usual" only deepens disengagement. Acknowledging grief helps employees begin to re-engage with their work:
   - ❖ Accept that productivity may dip in the immediate aftermath.
   - ❖ Check in with employees, not just about work, but about how they're adjusting.
   - ❖ Provide outlets for discussion, whether through team meetings, one-on-one conversations, or informal spaces to process together.

4. **Avoid Toxic Positivity.** In an attempt to keep morale up, some leaders resort to forced optimism and platitudes. *"We'll get through this!"* and

"Everything happens for a reason!" are not helpful. Let people feel what they feel. Instead of empty reassurance, offer grounded realism: *"I know this is hard, and I don't have all the answers, but I'm committed to getting through this with you."* Toxic positivity dismisses real pain:

- ❖ People don't need motivational slogans; they need honesty.
- ❖ It shuts down open conversations. Employees may feel pressured to suppress their frustration instead of working through it.
- ❖ It erodes trust. If leadership doesn't acknowledge hardship, employees feel like they're being asked to pretend everything is fine when it isn't.

5. **Provide Meaningful Support.** Employees need more than words; they need action. Help laid-off employees transition. Support remaining staff with realistic workloads and clear expectations. When leaders ignore the emotional toll of layoffs, they don't just harm individuals; they harm the entire institution:

- ❖ **For those laid off:** Offer real transition support: career services, networking connections, or severance packages.
- ❖ **For those remaining:** Clearly define expectations, redistribute work thoughtfully, and check in on workload balance.
- ❖ **For everyone:** Ensure access to mental health resources, whether through employee assistance programs, counseling, or peer support groups.

Chapter 2 Summary

Budget cuts aren't just financial decisions; they're deeply personal events that affect employees' identity, security, and well-being. Layoffs trigger grief, not just for those losing their jobs but also for those who remain, leading to fear, resentment, and disengagement. Organizations that fail to recognize the emotional toll of layoffs create workplaces where trust erodes, morale collapses, and long-term instability takes root.

In the next chapter, we'll focus on preparing for layoff conversations, including how to plan for communicating decisions clearly, handling emotional reactions, and ensuring that layoffs are carried out with dignity and fairness.

Chapter 2 Takeaways

- ❖ **Layoffs Trigger a Grief Cycle.** Job loss involves the same emotional stages as personal loss: denial, anger, bargaining, depression, and acceptance.
- ❖ **Remaining Employees Experience "Survivor's Guilt."** Those who stay often feel conflicted, overburdened, or anxious about their own future.
- ❖ **Fear Becomes the Dominant Workplace Emotion.** Uncertainty leads employees to withdraw, take fewer risks, and disengage.
- ❖ **Trust in Leadership Is Fragile.** Employees judge organizations not just by layoffs but also by how leadership handles them.
- ❖ **Trauma-Informed Leadership Is Necessary.** Recognizing distress and responding with empathy,

transparency, and fairness helps mitigate long-term damage.

Reflection: Recognizing the Emotional Impact of Layoffs

- ❖ How have past layoffs affected my organization's culture? Were the long-term effects fully acknowledged?
- ❖ What emotions am I seeing, or expecting, from my employees in response to recent or upcoming budget cuts?
- ❖ How do I plan to support both laid-off employees and those who remain?

Chapter 3
Prepare for Workplace Layoffs

---

*"Leadership is not about being in charge.
It is about taking care of those in your
charge."*
– Simon Sinek

There's no way to make layoffs easy. But there is a way to make them less harmful.

Layoffs don't just eliminate positions; they reshape an organization's culture, trust, and morale. They redefine how employees perceive leadership and whether they still believe the institution's values have stayed true to what they once were. Every conversation, every decision, and every omission matters.

That's why communication is just as important as the decisions themselves. Layoffs are not just about budgets. The way leaders frame the decision, deliver the message, and support both departing and remaining employees determines the long-term impact.

This chapter is about preparing for the difficult conversations ahead. Not just what to say, but how and when to say it. We'll also explore how leaders must prepare themselves emotionally to carry the weight of these decisions with steadiness and care.

Because in the end, layoffs are not only about who leaves. They are just as much about who stays and how we choose to lead them through what comes next.

Transparency Reduces Harm

Layoffs are painful, but the secrecy surrounding them makes them even worse.

I've learned that transparency doesn't eliminate pain, but it does reduce unnecessary harm. Uncertainty, secrecy, and vague justifications make layoffs unbearable. People don't have to like a decision to accept it, but they do need to understand it. They deserve to receive the message in a manner that shows them respect and dignity. When the process is clear and decisions are made with care, employees are more likely to move forward without lasting resentment.

Too often, leaders avoid being fully transparent because they fear that honesty will create more anger, more frustration, and more backlash. But withholding information doesn't prevent anger; it fuels it. When people don't understand the process, they fill in the gaps with their own assumptions. Rumors spread, and distrust grows. Trust that may have taken years to build can be lost in an instant.

I saw this firsthand during my second round of budget cuts, when I had to lay someone off for the first time. My leadership team and I were deep in difficult discussions. We were crunching numbers, weighing options, and making the best decisions possible with limited resources. We thought we were protecting employees by waiting until we had firm answers. But while we were immersed in the process, our staff was left in the dark.

Employees knew cuts were coming, but they had no insight into how decisions were being made. Uncertainty filled the vacuum we had created. Rumors spread about who was "safe" and who wasn't. Some lashed out, others withdrew, and morale across the organization began to erode. People didn't just fear losing their jobs; they felt powerless and disconnected from decisions that directly impacted their futures.

Secrecy doesn't just hurt those who lose their jobs; it damages the trust of those who remain. When employees feel excluded, when the process feels cold or arbitrary, resentment festers. The way we treat people in these moments becomes part of the institution's memory, something that endures long after the immediate crisis has passed.

By the time we were ready to communicate the decisions, the damage had already been done. Employees weren't only grieving the loss of their colleagues; they were also grieving the loss of trust in their leadership. Looking back, I realize that withholding information didn't protect anyone. It only deepened the harm.

No one expects layoffs to feel good, but they do expect leadership to be forthright, acknowledge the difficulty of the moment, and treat people with dignity. Transparency isn't about avoiding hard conversations; it's about ensuring that people feel respected and informed, even in the most challenging moments. And that's something I wish I had done better.

Lesson learned: Transparency is your greatest tool.

Transparency doesn't mean alarming people unnecessarily. It means respecting them enough to give them real information as soon as it's responsible to do so. It means making a commitment to share what is known when it's known rather than avoiding hard conversations until the last possible moment. It also means recognizing that layoffs don't just affect those losing their jobs. Those who remain are watching how leadership handles the process, and it will shape their trust in the institution long after the dust settles.

A transparent approach:

- ❖ **Signals respect.** Employees may not like the decision, but they will appreciate being treated as adults.
- ❖ **Gives people time to prepare.** Whether it's updating résumés, adjusting finances, or mentally preparing for change, time helps.
- ❖ **Maintains trust with those who remain.** When employees see layoffs handled clearly and honestly, they are less likely to feel that leadership is unpredictable or deceptive.

The key is to be honest without being reckless. Saying, *"Cuts are coming, but we don't know who yet,"* only fuels anxiety. Instead, explain the process's reasoning, the timeline, and when employees can expect firm answers.

Even when the news is bad, clarity is always better than uncertainty. Employees can handle hard truths far better than they can handle feeling blindsided.

Frame Layoffs in a Way That Feels Fair

Fairness isn't about making people happy, it's about helping them understand.

Employees are more likely to accept bad news when they can see the logic behind it. This doesn't mean they'll agree with the decision, but if they believe it was made through a fair and rational process, rather than arbitrary cuts or favoritism, they're less likely to respond with anger or resentment.

Some of the worst layoff experiences happen when leadership fails to explain why specific positions are being eliminated. When people don't understand the reasoning, they start filling in the gaps with their own assumptions:

"Maybe leadership is playing favorites."

"Maybe they're getting rid of the highest-paid employees to save money, regardless of their contributions."

"Maybe this is just an excuse to push out people they didn't like."

To prevent this, leaders need to be intentional about framing the decision and involve interested or affected parties in the process.

Plan with Intention, Communicate with Care

Transparency reduces uncertainty, but intentionality and early communication can provide employees with options and help reduce emotional intensity. I've seen firsthand how layoffs can trigger deep fear and resentment, but I've also learned that when people have even a small sense of agency, it can soften the impact.

We may not always be able to offer voluntary separations, severance, or financial incentives. But that doesn't mean we can't give employees some control over how they navigate the transition. How layoffs are handled can make the difference between employees feeling blindsided and disrespected or feeling considered and supported.

I learned this the hard way.

In my first round of staffing reductions, I focused on making the best decisions under difficult circumstances: ensuring the process was fair, treating those impacted with dignity, and handling communication with care. What I didn't fully appreciate was how much the process itself matters, not just for those leaving, but for everyone who remains.

One of my biggest missteps was assuming people only needed to know what was happening. In reality, they needed to understand *how* we got there. My leadership team and I wrestled with painful decisions behind closed doors, but because we weren't fully transparent, employees filled in the gaps themselves, with assumptions about favoritism, arbitrariness, and broken trust. Those assumptions caused far more damage than any official announcement.

Without a clearly communicated process, layoffs felt unpredictable. The remaining staff didn't just grieve the loss of colleagues; they worried they might be next. Some felt guilty about keeping their jobs. Others quietly began planning their own exits. The absence of information eroded trust more than the layoffs themselves.

I also underestimated the importance of timing. Because decisions had to be made quickly, employees had little time to prepare, deepening the sense of instability.

The second time around, I took a different approach.

I brought department heads into the process earlier. Instead of starting with a list of cuts, we followed a three-phase approach: first, we identified and prioritized the core services that had to be preserved; next, we streamlined those services to make them more sustainable; finally, we built staffing models around the essentials. This gave department heads a voice in shaping the outcome and helped us align reductions with our mission, rather than reacting in crisis.

I also communicated as early as possible, not just about the layoffs, but about the decision-making process itself. While the final budget numbers took time, I made sure employees in my area understood what was happening as soon as it was responsible to share.

This approach didn't erase the pain. But it created something that had been missing the first time: trust.

Employees knew the decisions had been thoughtful, that leadership wasn't operating in a vacuum, and that they had been treated with care, even when the outcomes were difficult.

Educate Yourself and Identify What You're Willing to Do

As a leader, you should be aware of the resources your organization has available to employees and whether they will be directly affected by any impending layoffs. This could help them prepare for their own next steps. Educate yourself in the following ways to the extent possible.

What resources are available at your organization? Collaborate with your HR staff to identify any available employee assistance programs, career resources, or other support services. Ensure you understand HR's procedures and policies and clarify roles and responsibilities.

Are internal transfers a feasible alternative to layoffs? If there are open positions elsewhere in the institution, collaborate with other leaders to identify possible connections, allowing affected employees to explore available options. This demonstrates that leadership is trying to minimize harm.

What external resources are available? While we may not always be able to provide severance, we can direct employees to career services, networking opportunities, resume workshops, and job search resources. This might include referrals to workforce development programs, professional associations, or industry-specific hiring networks. Don't neglect connections to other support services, such as employee assistance organizations that may be able to provide therapeutic services.

What are you willing to do? This could include serving as a positive reference, sharing relevant job postings, or directly connecting employees with hiring managers at other organizations.

Layoffs will always be painful, but leaders can mitigate unnecessary harm by approaching them with honesty, empathy, and a commitment to helping employees find new opportunities. Employees may not have control over the layoff decision itself, but they should feel supported in how they move forward.

Prepare Ourselves for Layoffs

As leaders, we spend a significant amount of time focusing on the logistics of layoffs, such as who will be affected, when announcements will be made, and what legal and HR requirements need to be met. As a result, we often forget to prepare ourselves emotionally. But layoffs are not just procedural; they're deeply personal for everyone involved, including those of us laying off our staff.

Layoffs trigger a wide range of emotions, not just for employees losing their jobs, but also for those who remain and for the leaders delivering the news. People may respond with grief, anger, disbelief, anxiety, or even relief. If we're not prepared for these reactions, we risk handling them poorly; becoming defensive when people lash out, shutting down when employees express frustration, or rushing through difficult conversations just to get them over with.

How Leaders Can Prepare Emotionally

Layoffs are not just an operational challenge; they are emotional ones. However, the way we handle these conversations and the way we show up emotionally will determine how employees process the news and how they remember us as leaders.

This section isn't about making layoffs easy. That's not possible. However, it is about ensuring you are prepared to handle them with the care, steadiness, and thoughtfulness they require.

Reflect on Your Own Reactions to Difficult Conversations

Before entering a layoff conversation, take a moment to assess how you typically respond to emotionally charged situations. Ask yourself:

- ❖ Do I avoid difficult conversations, hoping they will pass quickly?
- ❖ Do I over-explain in an attempt to make people feel better?
- ❖ Do I become detached, treating it as a purely transactional process?

Understanding your natural tendencies can help you anticipate potential missteps and adjust your approach. If you know you tend to rush through hard conversations, remind yourself to slow down. If you tend to over-explain, focus on delivering a clear, concise message. If you struggle with emotional conversations, practice what you'll say in advance so you don't freeze up in the moment.

This has been one of the hardest lessons for me as a leader. By nature, I'm pragmatic, forward-thinking, strategic, and focused on problem-solving. I prefer to complete tasks efficiently and move on to the next challenge. When I first arrived, I thought I had a quick fix for morale issues: addressing the concerns people voiced the most: low wages and a lack of professional development. But what I failed to see, and what they couldn't fully articulate at the time, was that their frustration ran much deeper. The years of constant cuts and a lack of transparency from former leadership had worn them down.

I came in with a vision and ideas, thinking that was what they wanted. That's what it appeared they were looking for during my interview. What they actually needed was my *emotional* support. Back then, I had a jaded perspective, assuming servant leadership and empathy were about doing good, not getting stuck in processing past institutional trauma. But I've since learned that staff morale isn't always just about moving forward; it can also be about recovering from the past. Staff and their emotional well-being are an institution's most valuable assets.

It took a lot of reflection and discernment to get here, and if you find yourself struggling with self-awareness in leadership, take the time to unpack it. It's worth it.

The more self-aware you are going in, the more prepared you will be to lead with intention.

Define Your Core Leadership Values

Layoffs will test you. In the moment, emotions will run high, both yours and those of the people receiving the news. The best way to ground yourself is to define your core leadership values beforehand. Ask yourself:

- ❖ Am I prioritizing transparency? Will I be upfront about why this decision is happening?
- ❖ Am I centering fairness? Will employees understand the reasoning behind the layoffs?
- ❖ Am I committed to compassion? Will I acknowledge the human impact of these decisions?

There is no "right" value set. Different leaders will approach layoffs differently. But if you don't define what matters to you ahead of time, you risk reacting in ways that don't align with your intentions.

When the conversation becomes difficult, and it inevitably will, your values should guide you.

Accept That Employees Will Have Emotional Reactions

No matter how well you prepare or how clearly you explain the decision, employees will still experience a range of emotions.

Some may cry. Some may be furious. Some may sit in stunned silence. Some may try to bargain, asking if there's any way to stay.

Their reactions aren't a reflection of you; they are a natural response to loss. However, as a leader, you must be prepared for them. Having a plan for how you will respond prevents you from reacting impulsively. It also allows you to meet employees where they are emotionally without losing sight of what they need from you: clarity, respect, and support. We'll discuss this more in Chapter 4.

Accept That You Will Feel the Weight of This Decision

Delivering layoff news isn't just hard on employees; it's hard on leaders, too.

No matter how necessary the decision is, it is painful to sit across from someone and take away their livelihood. You may feel guilt, exhaustion, or emotional fatigue. You may question whether you handled it the right way. You may carry the weight of the decision long after the conversation is over.

That's normal. And it's okay.

However, it's essential to acknowledge these feelings without letting them overshadow your responsibilities. Your job is not to make the pain disappear; it's to handle it with steadiness and care. If you need to process your own emotions beforehand, consider speaking with a trusted mentor, mental health professional, professional coach, HR professional, or colleague. If you enter these conversations carrying too much of your own emotional burden, supporting the people who need you will be more challenging.

Chapter 3 Summary

Layoffs are never easy, but the way they are communicated can make a significant difference in how employees process them. Secrecy and vagueness increase fear and distrust, while clear, honest communication helps employees prepare and reduces unnecessary harm. Leaders must also prepare themselves emotionally, anticipating how employees may react and ensuring their own ability to handle those responses with care and steadiness. Layoffs will always be painful. We cannot erase the loss or soften the reality of what they mean. But we can handle them with dignity, honesty, and fairness. After all, the goal isn't to make layoffs painless; it should be to make them as humane as possible.

In the next chapter, we'll discuss how to effectively deliver layoff conversations and deal with the fallout, as well as the different types of responses that may arise.

Chapter 3 Takeaways

- ❖ **Transparency Reduces Harm.** Employees can handle bad news better than uncertainty; leaders must communicate openly and promptly.
- ❖ **Framing Layoffs with Fairness Matters.** People don't need to agree with the decision, but they need to understand the reasoning behind it.
- ❖ **Layoff Conversations Are Emotionally Charged.** Leaders must be prepared to handle anger, grief, and bargaining and respond with clarity and empathy.

- ❖ **Remaining Employees Will Judge Leadership in this Moment.** How layoffs are handled significantly impacts long-term trust, morale, and employee engagement.
- ❖ **A Well-Prepared Leader Navigates the Process Effectively.** Emotional readiness helps ensure that the message is delivered with respect and confidence.

Reflection: Strengthen Your Approach to Layoff Conversations

- ❖ Have I clearly articulated why layoffs are happening and how decisions are being made?
- ❖ What questions or concerns do I anticipate from affected employees? How will I address them?
- ❖ How will I handle my own emotions when delivering difficult news?

Chapter 4
Communicate Workplace Layoffs

"People will forget what you said, people will forget what you did, but people will never forget how you made them feel."
– Maya Angelou

There's a moment, just before you come together with the employee in the room, when the weight of the conversation ahead fully settles onto your shoulders. You know what you have to say, but the enormity of it, and the fact that the news you are about to deliver will reshape someone's life in an instant, feels impossible to carry. And yet, as a leader, this is your responsibility.

No matter how well you prepare, delivering a layoff notice will never feel easy. There's no way to make someone's job loss painless. However, there is a way to mitigate its harm.

How you handle a layoff conversation affects not only the person on the receiving end of your message but also the employees who remain. If the message is delivered poorly, coldly, dismissively, or without clarity, it amplifies distrust.

Employees who feel blindsided or disrespected will leave with resentment, and those who stay will wonder whether they'll be treated the same way if, or when, their turn comes.

This chapter focuses on what I've learned about delivering a layoff notice with transparency, fairness, and dignity. It also outlines how to navigate various emotional responses, such as anger, shock, and grief, so that leaders can offer steady, compassionate guidance even in the most challenging moments.

Laying the Groundwork: Preparing for the Meeting

Layoffs are never just about numbers. They are about people. How you deliver the message will shape how those people process what's happening, not just in the moment, but in the days, weeks, and even the years ahead.

What to Consider Before the Meeting

Several factors should be considered before scheduling a one-on-one meeting to deliver a layoff notice.

- ❖ **Pick the right time.** Layoffs are best handled on a Tuesday or Wednesday, allowing employees to access HR and career resources while support is available. Avoid Fridays, as being laid off before the weekend leaves employees in limbo, unable to take immediate action or ask follow-up questions, making the experience even more isolating.
- ❖ **Allow sufficient time.** Plan to meet one-on-one for at least 30–45 minutes. Although some conversations may end sooner, avoid rushing.

- ❖ **Choose a private, neutral space.** If meeting in person, use an office or conference room to ensure confidentiality and dignity. If remote, a video call is more personal than a phone call.
- ❖ **Notify HR in advance.** Make sure all compliance and transition details are in place before meeting with the employee. This is also a good time to ensure you are aware of the HR support available for employees transitioning out of the organization.
- ❖ **Prepare your talking points.** Rehearsing what you plan to say with a trusted colleague or HR representative can help ensure that your message is clear and steady.

Delivering the News: A Framework for the Conversation

Layoff conversations should be conducted privately, directly, and respectfully. No one should ever find out they're losing their job through a group announcement or vague email.

How I try to structure the conversation

- ❖ **Start with clarity.** Be direct and avoid unnecessary buildup. Employees need to understand what's happening right away. For example: *"I have difficult news. Due to [reason], your position is being eliminated."*
- ❖ **Acknowledge the impact.** Recognize that this is a difficult moment. For example: *"I know this is hard, and I want to support you through this transition."*

- ❖ **Explain the next steps.** Provide clear information on severance, benefits, transition support, and any job placement assistance.
- ❖ **Allow space for emotions.** Some employees will ask questions, some may need silence, and others may react emotionally. Be prepared for anything.
- ❖ **Stay present.** Even if HR is involved in explaining logistics, your continued presence shows respect and care.

The worst thing you can do in these conversations is to hesitate or soften the truth too much. That lesson really hit home for me during a difficult firing, not a layoff, but a termination for performance issues. I knew the decision was the right one, but I dreaded the conversation. So, instead of being clear and direct, I over-explained. I walked through every issue, every documented warning, every attempt we had made to support improvement. I thought that if I laid out all the justifications, it would somehow soften the blow, that the employee would see the logic in the decision.

Instead, it had the opposite effect. The employee started debating each point, arguing that some of the issues weren't their fault, that they hadn't been given enough time, and that other people had made similar mistakes without consequences. I unintentionally turned the conversation into a negotiation by giving too many justifications. What should have been a brief but respectful discussion became drawn-out and painful for both of us. Worst of all, my hesitation and over-explaining made the employee feel even more blindsided and disrespected.

Afterward, I realized that clarity is a form of kindness. Whether it's a layoff or a performance-based termination, people deserve a direct and honest conversation, not a long-winded justification that makes them feel like they need to argue their case. The best thing you can do is be clear, acknowledge the difficulty, and provide support without trying to talk your way out of it.

Avoid long-winded explanations or excessive justifications. Keep it simple, acknowledge the difficulty, and provide support.

Handling Emotional Reactions

Every employee will process the news differently. Some may go silent, others may cry, and some may react with frustration or anger. How you respond to these reactions is important.

Know Your Limits: You're a Leader, Not a Therapist

You're responsible for delivering the message with compassion, but you're not responsible for mitigating the emotional fallout. Some employees will be devastated, and as much as you may want to ease their pain, you can't take full ownership of their emotional response. Your role is to deliver the message clearly and respectfully, to hold space for their emotions without taking it personally by becoming defensive or dismissive, and to help your employees connect to resources available at your organization.

Acknowledging the difficulty of the situation is okay, but avoid over-apologizing or making vague reassurances, such as *"I know you'll land on your feet"* or *"This is for the best in the long run."* While well-intentioned, these statements can come across as dismissive. Instead, focus on offering concrete support, such as severance details, career counseling, or networking opportunities. Refer your employees to professional resources, such as employee assistance programs, that can provide therapeutic support.

The following are examples of potential grief reactions to the news of a layoff, along with suggested leadership responses.

Denial: "This can't be happening. Are you sure?"

Some employees will struggle to accept the reality of their layoff. They may wonder if there was a mistake or assume there is still a way to reverse the decision. Others may sit in stunned silence, unable to process what's happening in the moment.

How to respond:

- ❖ **Acknowledge reality early and often.** Even if you don't have all the answers, be clear about what is happening and why.
- ❖ **Avoid false hope.** Offering vague assurances only prolongs the pain. People need the truth, even when it's difficult.
- ❖ **Provide space for people to process.** Some will need time to accept the situation, but clarity from leadership helps them begin that process.

- ❖ **Set expectations for what comes next.** Layoffs create uncertainty. Even if the future isn't fully clear, transparency about what leadership knows (and doesn't know) builds trust.

Recognizing denial isn't just about facing reality; it's about giving people the clarity they need to move forward, even in difficult times. And that's the first step toward rebuilding trust.

Anger: "This isn't fair!"

Some employees will react with frustration or even rage. They may lash out at leadership, the institution, or even at you personally. It's important not to take this personally. Anger is often a natural response to grief and loss.

How to Respond:

- ❖ **Stay calm and listen.** Allow them to vent without interrupting or becoming defensive. Sometimes, people just need to be heard.
- ❖ **Acknowledge their frustration.** Saying, *"I understand that this feels unfair"* or *"I hear that this is incredibly frustrating for you"* validates their feelings without escalating the conflict.
- ❖ **Reiterate the decision with empathy.** You can say, "I wish the situation were different, but this decision is final. I want to support you in any way I can as you navigate this transition."
- ❖ **Don't argue or justify excessively.** Over-explaining can make employees feel like they're being talked down to, rather than respected in their anger. Keep your message clear and steady.

Bargaining: "What if I take a pay cut or move to another department?"

Employees may try negotiating to keep their job by offering to take on extra work, switching to part-time status, or changing departments. While this is an understandable reaction, if the decision is final, it's important not to create false expectations.

How to Respond:

- ❖ **Be clear that the decision is final.** "I appreciate you looking for solutions, but unfortunately, this decision has already been made."
- ❖ **Acknowledge their willingness.** "I know you want to find a way to stay, and I want to help you with this transition."
- ❖ **Redirect to next steps.** Offer resources, job search support, or career coaching rather than leaving them feeling stranded.

Depression: "I don't know what I'm going to do."

For some, job loss feels like a personal failure. The emotional weight can be overwhelming, especially if they are worried about financial security, family obligations, or self-worth.

How to Respond:

- ❖ **Avoid empty reassurance.** Instead of saying, "You'll land on your feet," offer something concrete: "Here are some resources that may help with your next steps."

- ❖ **Offer immediate next steps.** Provide information about severance (if available), job search support, or connections to career counseling.
- ❖ **Give space for emotions.** If someone needs time to process, let them step away and follow up later.

Acceptance: "I understand. What happens next?"

Some employees will process the decision quickly and move into problem-solving mode. They may ask about logistics, benefits, and their final paycheck.

How to Respond:

- ❖ **Be prepared with details.** Have information ready on final paychecks, benefits continuation, and any available career resources.
- ❖ **Offer to help with references or networking.** A simple, *"I'd be happy to serve as a reference for you,"* can make a big difference.
- ❖ **End on a note of dignity.** Express gratitude for their contributions and acknowledge their impact on the organization.

Regardless of how employees react, how you handle their emotions will significantly shape their experience of the layoff. A difficult conversation doesn't have to be a damaging one. Thoughtful leadership in these moments can help people walk away feeling respected and supported, even in the face of job loss.

Layoffs will always be painful, but leaders can mitigate unnecessary harm by approaching them with honesty, empathy, and a commitment to helping employees transition smoothly. Although employees may not have control over the layoff decision itself, they should feel supported in their transition forward.

Communicating the Transition

Once the layoff conversation is over, your emotional work isn't done. In fact, it increases. Layoffs don't just affect the people being terminated; they leave a lasting impact on the team that remains and on you as a leader. How you handle the aftermath shapes trust, morale, and the organization's culture moving forward.

At this point, all eyes are on leadership. If employees see their colleagues being dismissed suddenly, without explanation or dignity, they'll assume the same could happen to them. Trust will erode, fear and disengagement will grow, and productivity and morale will suffer. On the other hand, if employees witness transparency, fairness, and care, they may not like the decision, but they'll feel more secure in leadership's integrity.

Hence, clear, compassionate communication becomes essential. Leaders should:

- ❖ **Acknowledge the loss.** Don't pretend nothing happened. Recognize that employees are losing colleagues, friends, and team members they relied on.
- ❖ **Be visible and available.** Leadership disappearing after layoffs signals indifference. Answer questions honestly, even when the answers aren't perfect.

- ❖ **Clarify expectations moving forward.** Employees will wonder how workloads will be redistributed and whether more cuts are coming. Address these concerns as openly as possible.

Leadership in these moments isn't just about those who were laid off; it's also about preserving trust in those who remain.

Take Care of Yourself as a Leader

Self-care is not a luxury; it's a necessity. Being responsible for managing the process leading up to layoffs is one of the most emotionally taxing responsibilities a leader can face. The stress of affecting people's livelihoods and the emotional reactions you will witness don't just disappear after the conversation ends. They linger, wearing you down if you don't take the time to acknowledge and process them.

It's easy to get caught up in the mindset that leadership means absorbing the burden alone; that because you make the decision, you have to carry it without showing strain. However, the truth is that leaders who neglect their own well-being aren't necessarily better leaders. They're just more depleted ones. And when you're depleted, you're less capable of providing the clarity, steadiness, and compassion that your team needs, both those who are leaving and those who remain.

Taking care of yourself doesn't mean dismissing the impact layoffs have on employees. It means recognizing that you cannot lead effectively if you're running on empty. It means giving yourself space to process, to reflect, and to seek support from those who understand the weight of leadership.

Chapter 7 will delve into practical self-care strategies in detail, covering topics such as managing stress and emotional fatigue, maintaining perspective, and seeking support in meaningful ways. But for now, the most important thing to remember is this: being a compassionate leader includes extending some of that compassion to yourself.

Chapter 4 Summary

Employees may not remember every detail of their time at your organization, but they will remember how they were treated when their job was taken away. Ask yourself:

- ❖ Did I treat them with dignity?
- ❖ Did I deliver the news with care or rush through it?
- ❖ Did I acknowledge the impact or act as if it was just a business decision?

People may not like what's happening, but they will always remember how it was handled. Your ability to approach this moment with empathy and clarity will shape how employees move forward, whether they walk away feeling abandoned or respected.

Delivering layoff news is one of the most challenging aspects of leadership and one of its most crucial responsibilities. People are an organization's greatest asset and should be stewarded with care. How leaders handle layoffs determines whether employees, both those who leave and those who stay, feel respected or discarded.

This chapter explored how to communicate job loss with transparency, empathy, and fairness, emphasizing the importance of directness, emotional awareness, and providing support during the transition.

In the next chapter, we'll focus on what happens after the layoff conversation. We'll look at how to support departing employees as they navigate their next steps. We'll then move on in Chapter 6 to focus on how to help remaining employees move forward in a changed workplace.

Chapter 4 Takeaways

- ❖ **Preparation Matters.** Layoff conversations should never be rushed or improvised. Planning ahead by choosing the right time, space, and approach ensures the message is delivered with thoughtfulness and care.
- ❖ **Clarity First.** Employees need a direct and unambiguous message. Avoid corporate jargon or excessive justifications. Confusion only adds to distress.
- ❖ **Acknowledge the Impact.** Layoffs trigger a range of emotions, including shock, anger, grief, and fear. Leaders must be steady, compassionate, and prepared for difficult reactions.
- ❖ **The Team is Watching.** How layoffs are handled affects more than just those being let go. It shapes the morale, trust, and culture of those who remain.

Reflection: Strengthening Your Layoff Conversations

- ❖ Have I prepared for this conversation in a way that respects the employee's dignity?
- ❖ How will I communicate the decision clearly and without ambiguity?
- ❖ Am I ready to respond to various emotional reactions with empathy and professionalism?

Chapter 5
Support Employees Who Leave

---

*"As we look ahead into the next century,
leaders will be those who empower
others." – Bill Gates*

Letting someone go is never just about the moment they hear the news. It's about everything that comes after: the uncertainty, the job search, the emotional fallout of losing not just a paycheck, but a daily routine, a professional identity, and a sense of belonging. And while you, as a leader, may not have control over whether the job remains, you *do* have control over how you support the person leaving.

Some institutions see layoffs as a clean break: deliver the news, process the paperwork, and move on. But that kind of transactional thinking ignores the real human cost of job loss. A better approach, one grounded in care and dignity, recognizes that how you support employees *after* they leave is just as important as how you handle the layoff itself.

This chapter isn't about making layoffs easier, because they won't be. Instead, it's about providing tangible ways to support employees through the transition and help them land on their feet.

Support Beyond Severance

Severance packages, when available, can provide short-term financial relief; however, they are rarely sufficient to replace a steady income. Even in institutions where severance isn't an option, there are key areas where leaders can provide practical help to offer meaningful support and help employees navigate the transition with dignity.

Frame the Exit: Help Employees Own Their Narrative

One of the most challenging aspects of losing a job is determining how to discuss it. The words a departing employee chooses to describe their layoff can shape their job search, confidence, and future opportunities.

Leaders can help employees frame their narrative in a way that acknowledges the reality of job loss while positioning them for success in their next role.

- ❖ **Acknowledge their strengths.** If an employee excels in project management, student engagement, community outreach, or any other area, reinforce that strength before they leave. What they contributed still matters, even if their job was cut.

- ❖ **Provide a neutral, professional explanation**. Instead of leaving departing employees to fumble through the *"Why did you leave your last job?"* question, offer language they can use in interviews. For example: *"Due to budget reductions, my position was eliminated along with several others. While I was sad to leave, I'm proud of the work I accomplished and am excited for my next opportunity."*
- ❖ **Help them highlight their impact.** Encourage employees to focus on accomplishments rather than just job duties. Instead of saying, *"I worked in student advising,"* they might say, *"I helped redesign our advising structure, improving student retention by 10%."*

Framing the exit this way helps the employee feel in control of their story rather than defined by circumstances beyond their control.

Offer References, Networking, and Moral Support

Once an employee is laid off, their professional network becomes one of their most valuable assets. Leaders can proactively contribute to that network by providing references, connections, and ongoing support.

- ❖ **Offer to be a reference.** If the employee's work was strong, tell them explicitly, "I would be happy to serve as a reference for you. Please don't hesitate to list my name and contact information."

- ❖ **Make introductions.** If you have connections in the employee's field, introduce them to people who may be hiring. A simple email can open doors.
- ❖ **Write LinkedIn recommendations.** A brief, positive recommendation on LinkedIn can boost their credibility with future employers.
- ❖ **Stay in touch.** Even a follow-up email a few weeks later to check in can mean a lot.

For many laid-off employees, the hardest part isn't just losing their job, it's feeling like they've been erased. Being in a position where they must ask for help can add insult to injury. A simple gesture on your part can help alleviate their burden, and letting them know they are still valued goes a long way.

Engage HR Without Dehumanizing the Process

HR plays a critical role in layoffs, ensuring compliance, processing benefits, and handling paperwork. But, in too many organizations, HR becomes a *barrier* rather than a *bridge*. The way HR interacts with employees can either reinforce their dignity or make them feel like they're just another number.

Be sure that you have a clear understanding of how your human resources department operates and what role they expect to play. They likely have specific processes in place. If not, it's your job as a leader to advocate for your employees. And there are several ways that you can work with HR to keep the process human-centered:

- ❖ **Advocate for exit meetings that are both supportive and procedural.** There should be a warm handoff to HR, where employees have the opportunity to ask questions, understand their rights, and feel heard.

❖ **Ensure clear communication**. Ensure employees understand their benefits, final paycheck details, and any available resources. Confusion adds stress.

❖ **Encourage HR to provide job transition resources.** Some organizations offer résumé workshops, career counseling, or job boards for former employees. If available, ensure the employee is aware of these options.

HR is often viewed as purely administrative, but when handled effectively, HR can be a key partner in ensuring employees receive the information and dignity they deserve.

Chapter 5 Summary

Layoffs don't end when an employee leaves. A leader's support for departing staff can significantly shape their transition and enhance their ability to move forward with confidence. The way leaders handle layoffs will be remembered long after employees are gone. Supporting employees doesn't erase the hardship, but it does help them to walk away with dignity, confidence, and a fair chance at what comes next.

In the next chapter, we'll focus on the remaining employees; those who are still processing what just happened, may be experiencing survivor's guilt, and are now looking to leadership for reassurance. Layoffs affect more than just those who are let go; they alter the entire culture of an organization.

Chapter 5 Takeaways

- ❖ **Help Employees Own Their Narrative.** Assist departing employees in framing their job loss in a way that allows them to explain their departure to future employers and maintain a sense of control over their career trajectory.
- **Offer Meaningful Support Beyond Severance.** Providing professional references, facilitating networking opportunities, and offering moral support can significantly improve an employee's transition. Ensuring they don't feel isolated during their job search reinforces that their contributions were valued.
- **Engage HR Without Losing the Human Element.** Thoughtful partnering with HR can help departing employees navigate the logistics with dignity and ensure the process remains compassionate and personal.

Not every institution can offer severance or financial aid. But every leader can offer care, respect, and tangible support.

Reflection: Help Employees Move Forward with Dignity

Supporting departing employees isn't just about checking boxes, it's about ensuring they have the best possible transition under difficult circumstances. Take a moment to reflect:

❖ How do I want employees to talk about their experience with my leadership after they leave?

❖ What practical resources, connections, references, résumé support, can I offer departing staff?

❖ Are there barriers in my institution (such as HR policies or a lack of networking opportunities) that prevent meaningful support? If so, what can I do to prepare for these before layoffs?

❖ If I were in their shoes, what kind of help would I want?

Chapter 6
Support Employees Who Stay

"Take care of your employees and they will take care of your business. It's as simple as that." – Richard Branson

---

Layoffs don't end when the last affected employee leaves the building. The impact lingers in the empty desks, the unanswered emails, and the way the air in the office feels just a little heavier. Those who remain are left to pick up the pieces, figuring out how to move forward in an organization that no longer feels quite the same.

For leaders, this moment is critical. It's easy to assume that, because employees still have their jobs, they will simply push ahead, relieved to have been spared. But that's not how people work. Layoffs shake institutional trust to its core, leaving behind survivor's guilt, burnout, and a lingering fear that the next round of cuts might be just around the corner. And if leaders fail to address these emotions head-on, the damage doesn't just disappear. It festers, leading to disengagement, resentment, and a workplace culture shaped by anxiety rather than purpose.

This chapter is about what happens "after." About what it means to lead a team that has been through loss. About the ways we can acknowledge pain without letting it define the future, rebuild trust without making empty promises, and move forward with a sense of hope, even when things are still uncertain.

The Emotional Aftermath: What Layoffs Leave Behind

At first, there's relief. The waiting is over. Employees know where they stand, and for a brief moment, that clarity provides a sense of stability. But then the reality sets in. The workplace is quieter, but not in a peaceful way. People hesitate before speaking up in meetings. Conversations feel strained. There's an unspoken tension, a collective uncertainty about what comes next.

Even those who once felt secure in their jobs now wonder if they really are. After all, their colleagues were just as dedicated, just as hardworking, just as essential. And then they were gone. The question lurks in the back of everyone's mind: *"If it happened to them, what's stopping it from happening to me…next time?"*

Survivor's Guilt: The Invisible Weight of Layoffs

Survivor's guilt is often one of the most overlooked yet deeply felt consequences of layoffs. Employees who remain may struggle with complex emotions, questioning why they were kept while others were let go. Some feel a sense of unfairness, wondering whether decisions were made arbitrarily. Others experience a deep, unsettling guilt, especially if they worked closely with those employees who lost their jobs.

This guilt can manifest in different ways:

- ❖ **Self-blame:** Some employees feel like they should have done more to help their colleagues, or they wonder if they somehow contributed to someone else losing their job.
- ❖ **Undeserved survival:** Others feel guilty that they were kept while others, sometimes more experienced or beloved colleagues, were let go. They struggle with a sense of "Why me?"
- ❖ **Mistrust and anxiety:** Many worry that one wrong move could put them next on the chopping block. They become anxious, overly cautious, and stressed about every decision.
- ❖ **Resentment and detachment:** Some employees pull back, not necessarily because they're angry at leadership, but because the workplace no longer feels like it once did. They feel disconnected and struggle to stay motivated.

Survivor's guilt doesn't just impact individuals; it reshapes team dynamics. Employees may feel hesitant to take on new responsibilities, fearing that doing so could be seen as benefiting from their colleagues' departures. Others may be reluctant to express excitement about future projects, worried that doing so will seem disrespectful to those who were let go. Team morale suffers as people grapple with how to move forward without erasing the loss they've experienced.

Uncertainty and silence from leadership can compound the weight of survivor's guilt. When no one talks about what happened, employees can make sense of it on their own. They may fill in the gaps with their own assumptions, often imagining the worst: more cuts are coming, they're next, and that their value to the organization is transactional at best.

Most leaders don't want employees to feel this way, but without direct acknowledgment and support, survivors' guilt festers. If left unaddressed, it can lead to disengagement, burnout, and a long-term erosion of trust in leadership and the institution itself.

Burnout: The Secondary Wave of Layoffs

While survivor's guilt weighs on employees emotionally, burnout takes a toll on them physically and mentally. Layoffs rarely result in a proportional reduction in workload. The work remains, even when the people don't. In many cases, that work is redistributed among those who are left.

At first, many employees will push through. They may even overextend themselves, feeling obligated to "make up" for the loss of their colleagues. But over time, the additional workload, combined with the emotional strain of survivor's guilt, can lead to exhaustion and disengagement.

Burnout doesn't just look like physical fatigue. It can manifest as:

- ❖ **Cynicism:** Employees become skeptical of leadership decisions, assuming future cuts are inevitable.
- ❖ **Emotional exhaustion:** Employees feel drained, unable to invest in their work the way they once did.
- ❖ **Reduced performance:** This is not always due to a lack of skill but to employees being stretched too thin and having trouble concentrating.
- ❖ **Withdrawal:** Employees disengage, doing only what's necessary to get by, avoiding extra responsibilities or collaboration.

If leaders don't acknowledge these realities, employees won't just move on. Instead, they will internalize their stress, keep their heads down, and quietly withdraw. Once that happens, rebuilding morale becomes much harder.

The good news? Leaders *can* make a difference in how people process and recover. But it requires intention, honesty, and a commitment to leading with care.

Rebuild Trust: Acknowledge Loss Without Getting Stuck in It

The weight of survivor's guilt, uncertainty, and burnout is especially heavy in the caring professions because the people we serve don't go away when our teams get smaller. The needs remain. For those who have dedicated their careers to service in fields like education, healthcare, social work, public health, or other mission-driven fields, this reality adds another layer of emotional strain.

Employees in these professions don't just mourn the loss of their colleagues; they also carry the weight of unfinished work, the clients or students who will feel the gaps, and the uncertainty of whether they can continue providing the same level of care with fewer hands. Responsibility doesn't disappear just because resources shrink; in fact, it often feels heavier. And when leadership missteps in communicating about these transitions, that weight only deepens.

I learned this firsthand. As I mentioned in the Introduction, during an earlier round of cuts, I thought I was offering support when I told employees that we needed to "do less with less." To me, it was a practical acknowledgment of reality. I thought that being open to focusing on less was a way to recognize that we couldn't maintain the same workload with a smaller team. But what my team heard was something entirely different.

They heard that all the work they had done before, everything they had poured their energy into, was now considered excessive, unnecessary, or easily discarded. They heard that their colleagues' contributions weren't valued, that the programs they built and the services they provided were things we could simply "do without."

That was never my intention, but that's how it landed. And I learned that how we frame these conversations matters just as much as the content of what we're saying.

Leadership has a responsibility to acknowledge reality without devaluing what came before. When teams are stretched thin, it's not a reflection of failure. It's not an indictment of those who remain or those who were let go.

It's simply a new reality that requires recalibration. The key is to make it clear that less doesn't mean lesser.

We must acknowledge that the work being done before mattered. It mattered then, and it still matters now, even if we have to shift priorities or scale things differently. The goal isn't to erase or diminish the past, but to ensure that moving forward is sustainable for those who remain.

Leaders who attempt to push forward as if nothing has changed risk alienating their teams even further. Ignoring the loss doesn't make it go away; it only creates an atmosphere where employees feel unseen, as though their work and their struggles are invisible. Instead, leadership must acknowledge the impact of layoffs in an open, honest, and compassionate way, while also helping their teams transition to a sustainable path forward.

Name the Loss, Openly and Honestly

Too many leaders make the mistake of pretending that layoffs are just another operational adjustment, something to be acknowledged briefly and then moved past as quickly as possible. But ignoring the emotional toll doesn't make it go away. It only tells employees that their feelings don't matter.

People need to hear their leaders acknowledge what happened. This doesn't mean dwelling on the pain, but it does mean recognizing that it exists. A simple statement can go a long way:

"I know these past few weeks have been hard. We've lost colleagues we valued, and the impact of that is real. I don't expect anyone to just move on overnight. It's okay to feel whatever you're feeling, whether that's sadness, frustration, or uncertainty. I want you to know that I see it, and I care about how we move forward together."

This kind of honesty does two things. First, it validates what people are experiencing. Second, it signals that leadership isn't trying to sweep things under the rug.

Employees don't need leaders to pretend that everything is fine. They need to know that what they're feeling is seen and understood. And they need to know that the work they're struggling to continue is still valued.

Create a Vision for the Future that Employees Can Rally Behind

Layoffs leave employees feeling unmoored. The organization they knew has changed, but what it's changing into isn't always clear. Without a sense of direction, people are left trapped in a state of uncertainty about what's expected of them or whether the institution is even on stable ground.

This uncertainty is even more pronounced in mission-driven work. When people dedicate their careers to serving others, they want to believe in the purpose behind their work. They want to know that their work still matters, that the mission still stands, even if the way they carry it out must change.

Leaders need to provide more than just reassurance. They need to offer a vision for the future, something employees can believe in.

This doesn't mean sugarcoating reality or making promises that can't be kept. Instead, it means being transparent about the organization's challenges while also defining a clear, meaningful path forward.

What a Rebuilding Vision Looks Like

The steps to rebuilding are simple. And they don't depend solely on you.

- ❖ **Clarify the mission moving forward.** If priorities have shifted due to budget realities, be clear about what they are. Employees need to know where to focus their energy.
- ❖ **Be honest about what's still uncertain**. It's okay not to have all the answers. If there are still unknowns, acknowledge them rather than pretending everything is settled.
- ❖ **Give employees a role in the rebuilding process.** Ask for their input. Involve them in shaping the next steps. People are more engaged when they feel like they have a say in the organization's future.
- ❖ **Help employees redefine success**. If doing more with less is unrealistic, help teams focus on impact over volume. This might mean shifting priorities, setting clearer boundaries, or accepting that some things will have to wait.

After our first round of layoffs, I saw the effects of survivor's guilt take hold. Some internalized the loss, while others grew mistrustful and anxious, wondering when the next cuts would come. Still others detached emotionally, struggling to invest in an organization they feared might not value them in return.

I could feel the cynicism setting in, and I knew I was not immune to it. As the face of leadership, I became an easy target for frustration, even from those I had worked hard to support. There was no easy fix. However, one thing became clear: if we were going to move forward, people needed a way to envision themselves in the institution's future again.

Instead of dictating a new direction from the top down, I shifted my focus. I asked departments and teams to help me create it. Together, we built a committee- and department-driven strategic direction document. It was not a sweeping plan full of unattainable promises. Instead, it mapped out tangible goals we could strive toward, even in the midst of uncertainty. It offered a direction that employees could shape and own.

That co-creation process made all the difference. It gave people a reason to reengage, not because they were told to, but because they had helped imagine the path forward. It didn't erase the grief or frustration overnight, but it offered something meaningful to rally behind: a future they had helped shape. It was a good start and began to shift the dynamics of trust, soften the edges of cynicism, and help us start rebuilding together.

But a vision that employees can rally behind doesn't have to be a grand strategy document. It can be as simple as:

"We are in a period of transition, but our mission remains the same. Our work still matters. In the coming months, I look forward to hearing from you—your ideas, concerns, and what you need from me as we navigate this together.

You are not just employees; you are the heart of this institution, and we will move forward as a team."

Recognize and Celebrate Employees Without Invalidating Loss

One of the most challenging tasks in the aftermath of layoffs is striking a balance between acknowledging loss and moving forward. Leaders need to show appreciation for the employees who remain, but if done carelessly, this can backfire.

Employees don't want to hear, *"You're lucky to still have a job."* That's not gratitude, it's a reminder of their vulnerability. They also don't want to hear forced optimism, as if everything is fine when it isn't.

And yet, recognition matters. Remaining employees need to feel that their contributions are recognized and valued, not just as bodies filling gaps, but as individuals who continue to do meaningful work.

Ways to Show Appreciation Thoughtfully

Finding the right balance between honoring loss and recognizing effort isn't easy. Employees don't expect perfection from leadership. But they expect and deserve honesty, care, and a willingness to listen. Make the effort. Some ways that you can do that include:

- ❖ **Recognize extra effort.** Many employees will be taking on additional responsibilities. Acknowledge it explicitly: *"I know this has been a heavy lift, and I* *appreciate everything you're doing to keep things moving."*

❖ **Make gratitude specific.** Instead of generic thank-yous, highlight real contributions: "I saw how you stepped up to cover X after the restructuring, and I want you to know that it hasn't gone unnoticed."

❖ **Create space for collective reflection.** Give employees the opportunity to discuss what they need moving forward. Whether through team meetings or individual check-ins, the message should be: *"I value your perspective, and I want to make sure we're supporting each other."*

By acknowledging loss, providing a meaningful vision for the future, and offering thoughtful recognition, leaders can help employees navigate this transition, not by erasing the past, but by honoring it as they build toward what comes next.

Chapter 6 Summary

Layoffs affect not only those who lose their jobs but also those who remain. If not addressed, survivors' guilt, burnout, and uncertainty can take hold, reshaping workplace culture and eroding trust. Employees in caring professions grieve their colleagues but also worry about the work left undone, the long-term stability of the organization, and whether they're next in line for cuts.

Leaders who fail to acknowledge this reality risk creating a disengaged, fear-driven workplace, where employees operate out of self-preservation rather than shared purpose. However, leaders who respond with honesty, transparency, and care can help teams process the loss, rebuild trust, and reframe their work in a way that feels meaningful and sustainable.

Leadership isn't just about making tough decisions; it's about guiding people through the aftermath. In the next chapter, we'll focus on navigating ongoing uncertainty while sustaining morale and engagement. Layoffs may end, but their impact lasts far beyond the initial transition.

Chapter 6 Takeaways

- ❖ **Survivor's Guilt is Real.** Employees may struggle with guilt, resentment, or detachment. If left unaddressed, these emotions undermine morale and productivity.
- ❖ **Burnout is the Secondary Wave of Layoffs**. Workloads don't decrease just because staff do. Without intentional support, employees will stretch themselves too thin.
- ❖ **Acknowledge Loss Openly.** Ignoring layoffs doesn't make them disappear; it tells employees that their experiences don't matter.
- ❖ **Frame Change Without Devaluing Past Work.** Employees need to hear that their contributions, and those of their former colleagues, still matter.
- ❖ **Create a Vision Employees Can Rally Behind.** A clear, realistic path forward helps employees feel engaged and connected to the mission.
- ❖ **Recognize and Celebrate Remaining Employees Thoughtfully.** Appreciation must be genuine and specific. not just a reminder that they are "lucky" to still have a job.

❖ **Rebuilding Trust Takes Time.** Consistency, honesty, and a willingness to listen are critical to helping employees move forward.

Reflection: The Message You Send to Those Who Remain

Layoffs are a turning point for any organization, but how leadership responds determines whether employees regain trust or quietly check out.

❖ How am I acknowledging the emotional impact of layoffs on my team?

❖ What steps am I taking to ensure that employees feel valued and not just "lucky" to be employed?

❖ Am I helping employees redefine success in a way that makes sense for a smaller team?

❖ Does my communication about the future feel transparent and realistic, or vague and disconnected?

❖ How am I ensuring that recognition feels authentic, not performative?

Chapter 7
Support Yourself as a Leader

---

*"You cannot lead others until you first
lead yourself." – John C. Maxwell*

Leadership can be lonely. The higher you rise in an organization, the fewer peers you can lean on. And that loneliness deepens when you're the one making the tough decisions. Especially when those decisions involve layoffs or restructuring.

People often assume that leaders have a certain level of detachment, making difficult choices with a pragmatic distance. But for those of us who lead with care and compassion, that's not how it works. The weight of these decisions lingers. The impact on people's lives stays with us. We worry and fret. These decisions keep us up at night. And in moments of doubt, we wonder: *"Did I do enough? Did I handle this correctly? Could I have found another way?"*

The reality is that leading well requires emotional labor: a quiet, unseen burden that accumulates over time. Servant leaders, in particular, are deeply invested in the well-being of their employees and the communities they serve. That investment is what enables us to excel at what we do.

However, it also means we carry the guilt, grief, and responsibility long after everyone else has moved on.

The challenge is that ethical leadership requires emotional sustainability. If we don't take care of ourselves by setting boundaries, building resilience, and allowing ourselves space to process the weight of our choices, we risk burnout. And a burned-out leader can't lead with care.

This chapter is about what happens during and after the hard decisions have been made and how we care for ourselves so we can continue to care for others.

The Unseen Burden of Tough Decisions

Making hard choices comes with a cost. There's no getting around it. When you decide to lay off employees, restructure a unit, or cut a program, it's not just a line-item adjustment; it's the impact on individual lives and livelihoods. Even when you know the decision was necessary, it isn't easy.

For many leaders, the hardest part isn't making the decision itself, it's the aftermath. It's walking into work the next day, feeling the weight of the loss. It's wondering if, or how, people see you differently now. It's knowing that some employees blame you, whether or not they say it out loud. And sometimes, you blame yourself.

This is the part of leadership no one talks about. It's how you carry the emotional weight of the decision alone.

Your team has each other. They can commiserate, process, and grieve together. But you? You are the leader.

And leadership, by its nature, is isolating.

Even if you have a leadership team, you may all be processing this type of burden differently. Few friends or family outside of work can fully grasp the complexity of the choices you make every day. As a leader, you often feel stranded on an island.

This is why taking care of yourself isn't a luxury; it's a necessity. As a leader, you must intentionally build a support system and create space to process the weight of your role.

The Emotional Labor of Leadership

People often discuss leadership in terms of strategy, vision, and decision-making, but they rarely address the topic of grief.

Layoffs, restructuring, budget cuts. These aren't just operational adjustments. They are losses. And loss requires mourning.

But here's the hard part: as a leader, you don't always get the space to grieve. You are expected to be steady, to hold everything together, to guide your team forward. And while that's certainly part of the job, you aren't immune to the emotional impact of what's happening.

Leadership comes with an emotional toll when you care deeply about your work and the people you serve. Doubt, guilt, and exhaustion are natural responses to difficult decisions. The problem is that too many leaders ignore these feelings, telling themselves to just keep moving forward.

However, suppressing emotions doesn't make them disappear. They accumulate. And if you don't create space to process them, they manifest in unhealthy ways: burnout, cynicism, disengagement.

The truth is, leaders need care, too. Not just from others, but from themselves.

You've heard it before, on every airplane: "Secure your own oxygen mask before assisting others."

This simple instruction carries a deeper truth, one that applies to leadership just as much as it does to air travel. If you don't take care of yourself first, you won't be able to help anyone else effectively.

The idea that leaders must always put others first is a dangerous one. Yes, leadership requires sacrifice. Yes, leadership means making difficult choices. But leadership is also about sustainability.

If you ignore your own well-being, if you push yourself past the point of exhaustion, you don't become a better leader; you become a depleted one. Burned-out leaders make reactive decisions, struggle to communicate clearly, and lose the ability to be emotionally present for their teams.

Taking care of yourself isn't indulgent, it's responsible. Just as you would put on your own oxygen mask first, prioritizing your own well-being ensures that you have the capacity to support others effectively. Self-care is the foundation of ethical leadership because it enables you to lead with clarity, resilience, and compassion over the long term.

So what does that actually look like in practice?

Strategies for Resilience

Leaders who sustain themselves through challenges don't just "power through." They build intentional habits that allow them to process, reflect, and recharge.

Set Boundaries to Prevent Burnout

Leadership can consume every part of your life if you let it. Setting boundaries isn't about neglecting responsibilities; it's about ensuring that your work doesn't eclipse your ability to function as a whole person.

- ❖ **Create mental separation.** Establish times when you disconnect from work completely: no emails, no office chat messages, no late-night *"just checking in."*
- ❖ **Don't take on everything yourself.** You cannot, and should not, carry the weight of every problem alone. Delegate. Trust your team.
- ❖ **Protect your personal time.** Whether it's exercise, reading, family time, or hobbies, make sure to have something in your life that exists outside of your leadership role.

Find Mentors and Peer Support Networks

Leadership can be isolating, but it doesn't have to be lonely. The higher you rise in an organization, the fewer peers you have who truly understand the pressures you face. That's why finding people who get it, who have walked this path before or are walking it alongside you, is critical.

Seek Out Mentors

A mentor isn't just someone with more experience. They're a guide who can help you see past immediate challenges. They remind you that your struggles aren't unique; others have been through similar experiences, and you will make it through. A good mentor offers perspective, wisdom, and sometimes just the reassurance that you're not alone in the weight of leadership. I was fortunate to have leveraged a mentorship through the doctoral program I completed prior to starting this position. Professional associations, alumni organizations, or other networking resources may have similar programs.

Join Peer Groups

While mentors provide guidance based on their experience, peers offer solidarity in the present. Whether within your industry or beyond it, connecting with other leaders who are actively navigating similar challenges can be invaluable. These conversations don't need to be formal. Sometimes, they happen over coffee, in online forums, or through professional associations. What matters is having a space where you can speak openly about the realities of leadership without needing to filter your words.

Seek Professional Support

Leadership during layoffs and budget cuts carries a heavy emotional burden, and it's not something you have to navigate alone. Seeking professional support, whether through therapy, coaching, or peers, can provide essential guidance and relief.

- ❖ **Employee Assistance Programs (EAPs).** Many workplaces have EAPs, but not everyone realizes what they actually offer. These programs provide employees with free, confidential access to short-term counseling, stress management tools, and financial advice. Whether you're dealing with the stress of layoffs, feeling overwhelmed by leadership decisions, or just need someone to talk to, an EAP can be a great resource to help you navigate tough transitions.
- ❖ **Therapy and Counseling.** Speaking with a licensed therapist can help process the emotional toll of leadership, including feelings of guilt, stress, and burnout. Therapy provides a structured space to navigate difficult decisions while maintaining your well-being.

Seeking professional support isn't a sign of weakness; it's a strategic investment in your well-being. When you care for yourself, you're better equipped to care for those who rely on your leadership.

Have Honest Conversations

Leadership comes with constant decision-making, and not all of those decisions will be easy, or popular. Having a trusted network where you can talk through dilemmas, express doubts, and receive honest feedback is essential. The key is to find people who will listen without judgment but also challenge you when needed. The best support network doesn't just reassure you, it helps you grow.

Practice Mindfulness, Reflection, and Discernment

Good leadership calls for more than quick decisions; it requires presence, awareness, and thoughtful action. Mindfulness helps leaders stay grounded in the present moment, creating space between stimulus and response. Reflection allows leaders to look back with honesty, learning from both successes and missteps. And discernment guides leaders forward, ensuring that choices are made with care, integrity, and alignment with deeper values. Together, these practices help leaders navigate complexity with greater steadiness and purpose.

Center Yourself in Mindfulness

Effective leadership starts with being steady under pressure. Mindfulness isn't about perfection or detaching from reality; it's about building the mental resilience to stay present, think clearly, and respond intentionally. Before you can reflect honestly or make wise decisions, you need enough mental space to see situations as they are.

Even a few minutes of focused breathing or quiet can help you approach challenges with more clarity and composure. Mindfulness doesn't require major changes; it starts with small habits that strengthen your ability to lead with calm and focus, especially when it matters most. It can be as simple as doing one of the following:

❖ **Take a moment to reset with 4-7-8 breathing.** Before stepping into a difficult conversation, pause and practice the 4-7-8 breathing method. Inhale deeply through your nose for a count of 4, hold your breath for a count of 7, and then exhale slowly through your mouth for a count of 8. Repeat this cycle three times. This simple practice can lower stress, clear mental clutter, and help you enter the conversation with greater calm, focus, and presence.

❖ **Do a body scan before bed to release tension built up during the day.** Lie down in a comfortable position and mentally check in with each part of your body, starting from your toes and moving up to your head. Notice any areas of tightness or discomfort, and consciously relax them as you breathe deeply. This practice can help ease muscle tension, quiet the mind, and prepare you for more restful sleep.

❖ **Create a transition ritual between work and home.** Try a five-minute meditation or listening to calming music before stepping into your personal life. Instead of carrying the stress of the workday into your evening, set a clear boundary with a simple ritual. On your commute, take five minutes to sit quietly, practice deep breathing, or listen to relaxing music. This small but intentional shift signals to your brain that work is done, helping you be more present for yourself and those around you.

Reflection through Journaling

Mindfulness helps us stay steady in the moment. But making sense of our leadership over time requires reflection. Reflection isn't about perfection or judgment, it's about learning. Writing things down, even briefly, can reveal patterns we might miss in the rush of daily decisions.

For me, this book is an act of reflection. Writing about my experiences has helped me process difficult decisions, recognize my blind spots, and clarify what I want to carry forward in my leadership.

You don't have to write a book, but keeping a journal, even if it's just a few bullet points a day, can provide a space to sort through complex emotions and identify patterns in your leadership approach.

Journaling can help with:

- ❖ Processing emotions instead of letting them fester.
- ❖ Identifying patterns in decision-making and leadership style.
- ❖ Recognizing growth over time to help you see progress, even when leadership feels like an uphill climb.

Leadership is ongoing. The challenges shift, the decisions evolve, but the weight of responsibility remains. Creating a weekly, monthly, or even quarterly structured reflection practice helps ensure you lead with intention, rather than reacting to circumstances.

If you're not sure where to start, try a simple prompt: "What's one leadership decision I made today that I feel proud of? What's one I wish I had handled differently?"

Go Deeper: Building Leadership Discernment

Reflection through journaling helps us process and learn from our experiences. But to take that self-awareness one step further, leaders can practice structured discernment, a daily or weekly check-in designed to reconnect actions with values.

- ❖ Where did I feel most aligned with my values today?
- ❖ Where did I feel most challenged or unsettled?
- ❖ What am I most grateful for?
- ❖ What would I want to carry forward into tomorrow?

This practice isn't about judgment; it's about noticing patterns over time. Moments of clarity, moments of drift, and the subtle course corrections that build stronger leadership.

Even a few minutes of intentional discernment helps you reconnect your daily actions to your larger purpose. Over time, this habit strengthens your ability to notice when you're aligned and when you're not, making adjustments a natural part of your leadership. Ultimately, what distinguishes reactive leadership from intentional leadership is a crucial yet straightforward discipline: the willingness to pause, reflect, and adapt.

Mindfulness, reflection, and discernment are not luxuries reserved for quiet moments. They're the tools that steady us in the hardest moments. They help us lead with honesty, stay grounded in our values, and build the resilience needed to navigate uncertainty. Together, they create the foundation for leadership that is thoughtful, courageous, and sustainable for ourselves and for those we serve.

Chapter 7 Summary

Leadership comes with an unseen burden, the weight of making difficult decisions, the emotional toll of serving others, and the isolation that comes with higher-level responsibilities. The more responsibility you carry, the fewer peers you have who truly understand what you're going through. While leaders are expected to support their teams, they often struggle to find the same level of support for themselves.

This chapter emphasized the importance of self-care, not as an indulgence, but as an ethical responsibility. Burned-out leaders make poor decisions, lead reactively, and struggle to be fully present for their teams. Taking care of yourself isn't selfish; it's essential to sustain effective and compassionate leadership.

To build resilience and prevent burnout, leaders must:

- ❖ Set boundaries to prevent work from consuming their lives.
- ❖ Find mentors and peer support networks to avoid isolation.
- ❖ Practice discernment and reflection to stay grounded in their values.

Leadership is a long-term commitment, not a short sprint. By taking care of yourself, you ensure that you can continue to lead with clarity, integrity, and compassion. True leadership isn't just about showing up for others; it's about ensuring you have the capacity to keep showing up in the long run.

Chapter 7 Takeaways

* ❖ Leadership is isolating, but it doesn't have to be lonely. Finding mentors and peer support is essential.
* ❖ **The emotional labor of leadership is real.** Carrying responsibility for others can lead to guilt, doubt, and burnout if not managed.
* ❖ **Self-care is an ethical responsibility.** Leaders who neglect themselves lead from exhaustion rather than clarity.
* ❖ **Setting boundaries is not neglecting responsibility.** It ensures sustainability and prevents leadership from overshadowing personal well-being.
* ❖ **Reflection helps leaders stay intentional.** Journaling, mindfulness, and structured check-ins keep leadership decisions aligned with values.

Reflection: How Are You Caring for Yourself as a Leader?

Leadership isn't just about guiding others. It's about sustaining yourself in the face of the weight of responsibility. Take a moment to reflect:

* ❖ How have past difficult decisions affected me emotionally and mentally?
* ❖ Do I have strategies in place to prevent leadership burnout?
* ❖ Who are my trusted peers, mentors, or support networks?
* ❖ What is my plan for processing stress and maintaining emotional sustainability?

Chapter 8
Plot Twist!

"The ultimate measure of a leader is not where they stand in moments of comfort and convenience, but where they stand at times of challenge and controversy."
– Martin Luther King Jr.

When I first started writing this book, I thought I knew exactly what I was working through: how to lead through layoffs with care, how to support employees through transitions, and how to navigate the weight of these decisions with integrity.

But leadership is never just theoretical. Life has a way of turning lessons into lived experiences.

I set out to write about leadership, but the most profound revelation ended up being about my own journey.

Am I Still What This Institution Needs?

Through the extreme budget cuts my institution faced, I was forced to reckon with a question I hadn't fully considered: If we are prioritizing positions and services that provide the most direct support for students, where does that leave me?

Here's the truth: In this role, I was almost entirely focused on administration and external engagement. I wasn't teaching, and I wasn't providing direct student services. My strengths are in vision, strategy, budgeting, and grant writing. Skills that are vital not only during times of growth but also in shaping a thoughtful response to contraction. Yet in a moment defined by urgent triage and institutional survival, there was less space to apply the kind of long-range thinking and systems-level planning that I do best. Especially when my research areas and strategic priorities were among those most vulnerable to federal cuts.

I realized that the most ethical leadership decision I could make was to scrutinize my own position, as we had scrutinized every other. If I were asking others to sacrifice, accept a leaner structure, and shift priorities, how could I not be willing to do the same?

And so, I had to ask myself a hard question: "In this current moment, am I what this institution needs most?"

The answer wasn't easy. I had spent the previous two years honing my leadership philosophy, working to bring stability and strategic vision to the institution through multiple rounds of significant cuts. But when I took a step back and looked at the budget numbers, the reality was clear: My position was a substantial financial cost at a time when every dollar counted.

I'd been thinking about the necessity of a purely administrative Dean for a while, and my department heads only reinforced this idea during an emergency budget retreat. As I kept steering the conversation back to a focus on core services that directly impacted student success, someone finally asked, "So if that's what really matters, what core services are provided by the Dean's Office?" It was one of the rare moments when we were all on the same page. While I didn't fully let on that I shared their perspective, I assured them I would bring the question to the Provost.

A Conversation I Never Expected to Have

Up to this point, this book has emphasized the importance of protecting the people who do the work, the ones who keep institutions functioning even in times of crisis. But in this moment of decision, I had to take my own advice. If we were prioritizing student-facing roles, leadership couldn't be exempt. Limited resources needed to go where they had the greatest impact. In good conscience, my own role needed to be on the table when that budget line could preserve multiple positions directly tied to student support.

So, I sat down with my Provost and initiated a conversation I never thought I'd have:

"I want to discuss whether my unit needs an administratively focused dean. And if it doesn't, then we need to be honest about that, even if it means restructuring my role out of existence."

I didn't make the decision lightly. My career had been built on strategic leadership, external partnerships, and long-term institutional planning. But in that moment, facing a new budget reality, it was clear the university needed a renewed focus on its core work, with leadership closer to that work rather than adding more layers of administration. Our conversations shifted from budgets to what it truly meant to meet the moment with clarity and purpose, and how we could create a leadership model that was more efficient, sustainable, and aligned with the institution's evolving needs.

A Strategic Shift Toward a Flatter, More Operational Leadership Structure

After much discernment and with feedback from my department heads, we agreed on the following changes:

- ❖ The academic Dean role would be restructured into a director-level position with a more operational focus.
- ❖ Instead of serving as a vision-driven, outward-facing leader, the new role would emphasize internal operations and be filled by a department head on a two-year rotating basis, similar to a Department Chair.

Appointing someone from within the institution would provide continuity, drawing on the knowledge and trust already built with the unit, campus, and community. My position was redistributed, and just like that, my time as Dean came to an end.

This wasn't just a budget-cutting decision; it was an intentional move toward flattening the administrative hierarchy, reducing bureaucracy, and placing leadership closer to day-to-day operations. By streamlining the leadership structure, we created a more responsive and integrated model. It was a model that empowered the people doing the work.

This shift also represented a broader trend across higher education, an acknowledgment that administrative overhead needs to be carefully scrutinized. Institutions were no longer in a period of expansion; they were in a period of consolidation and adaptation. By flattening leadership roles, we were positioning the institution to prioritize its core mission while creating a model that was more agile, more sustainable, and more connected to the people it served.

A Practical and Ethical Shift in Leadership

We weren't just saving money by moving to a rotating leadership model filled by internal candidates. We were choosing leaders who had already earned the trust of their colleagues, who understood the institution's challenges firsthand, and who would be seen as long-standing partners rather than as enforcers of external mandates. We chose continuity, trust, and the preservation of institutional knowledge.

In times of crisis, trust in leadership is just as important as financial stability. If people don't believe that leadership understands their struggles, morale erodes and disengagement sets in. By flattening the hierarchy and placing leadership closer to the work, we made a statement: decisions should not be made from an ivory tower, but from within the community they impact.

Building a More Sustainable Leadership Model

This decision also created a leadership model that was better suited for the institution's immediate future. In times of financial strain, institutions cannot afford leadership that exists only for the sake of leadership. The most effective leadership is functional, flexible, and directly tied to mission-critical work.

By restructuring:

- ❖ We ensured that leadership was directly engaged with the people and the work.
- ❖ We eliminated unnecessary administrative layers, creating a more efficient structure.
- ❖ We reinvested savings into the people who have the most direct impact on students.
- ❖ We modeled the kind of institutional adaptation that will be necessary in the years to come.

For me, this decision reinforced one of the most challenging but most valuable lessons of leadership: We can't ask others to change if we are not willing to change ourselves.

There is often resistance to rethinking leadership structures. Not because people are unwilling, but because change is hard, and leadership roles carry a sense of prestige, stability, and authority. But titles are not what make leadership effective; actions are.

In the end, stepping into a leaner leadership model was not about loss; it was about alignment. It was about ensuring that the institution was structured in a way that best served its mission, not its hierarchy. It was about leading with integrity, not by preserving roles, but by ensuring that leadership is truly essential, functional, and sustainable.

Because in times of crisis, leadership isn't just about making decisions from above. It's about ensuring that the right people are in place to move the institution forward, not just in theory, but in the lived reality of those who remain.

The Journey Through Hard Decisions

In writing this book, I've walked through every painful step of what ethical, compassionate leadership looks like in times of crisis.

We started by understanding the human cost of layoffs, recognizing that behind every budget cut is a person with a life, a career, and a future now uncertain. We examined how to communicate layoffs with care, ensuring that even in the most difficult moments, we treat people with dignity and respect. We explored how to support both departing employees and those who remain, acknowledging that layoffs don't just affect the individuals leaving; they reshape an institution's culture and morale.

We discussed the emotional toll of leadership, the quiet burden of being the one who makes the decisions, and the importance of taking care of ourselves so that we can continue to lead with integrity.

And now, we arrive at perhaps the hardest lesson of all: true leadership isn't about holding on to authority, it's about recognizing when the institution's needs have changed and having the courage to make the difficult decisions that best serve those who remain, even when those decisions include yourself.

Final Reflection: What Kind of Leader Do You Want to Be in Hard Times?

Leadership in a mission-driven, caring organization should never be about authority or self-preservation. It should be about stewardship by ensuring that the people, mission, and values that define the institution remain strong, even when faced with difficult choices.

Organizations committed to the public good, whether in education, healthcare, social services, or community work, exist for a purpose larger than themselves. They are built to serve, uplift, and provide stability and opportunity to those who depend on them. Yet these organizations often face the harshest realities in times of crisis.

In these moments, leadership isn't just about making choices. It's about ensuring those choices reflect the values we claim to uphold.

There will come a time in your leadership journey when you must decide what kind of leader you truly are. Not in theory, but in the real, often painful work of shaping the future. You may have to determine which programs to cut, which positions to eliminate, or how to sustain an institution with fewer resources but no fewer responsibilities.

This is when leadership is tested. Not by what's easy, but by what's right.

As you navigate these challenges, I leave you with these questions:

- ❖ **When faced with difficult decisions, how will you ensure your choices align with your values?** It's easy to lead with integrity when times are good. It's much harder when every option carries a cost. What principles will anchor you when no solution feels ideal?
- ❖ **How will your actions shape the future culture of your organization?** Every decision sets a precedent. Will your choices leave behind a hollowed-out institution, or one where trust and purpose endure?
- ❖ **Are you willing to scrutinize your own role with the same fairness you apply to others?** If your organization were rebuilding from the ground up, would your position still be essential? And if not, what does integrity ask of you?
- ❖ **How do you lead so that, years from now, you can look back and know you did the right thing?** Not an easy thing. Not the self-protective thing. The right thing for the people and the mission you serve.

Those who work in caring organizations don't do it for the wealth or status, but because they believe in something greater. As leaders, we're entrusted with more than budgets and policies; we're entrusted with preserving that belief.

And sometimes, the greatest act of leadership isn't about holding on. It's about making space and ensuring the institution can endure and thrive, even if that means stepping aside.

Because leadership in service to others is never about the leader. It's about the mission, the values, and the people who remain long after we are gone.

Layoffs will never be easy. But how we handle them matters:

- ❖ Lead with honesty.
- ❖ Treat people with dignity.
- ❖ Make decisions that align with your highest values.

And above all, lead in a way that lets you look back with clarity, knowing you chose care and compassion over convenience.

Checklist for Layoffs With Care and Compassion

This checklist is designed to help you navigate layoffs with transparency, care, and compassion. Use it in conjunction with the strategies in this book to manage the logistical and emotional challenges of layoffs while preserving trust and minimizing harm to your organization's culture.

Step 1: Reflect on Your Leadership Values & Objectives

Purpose: Clarify why you are making these decisions and what kind of leader you want to be.

Action Items:

☐ **Identify Your Core Values:** Write down the leadership values you want to honor and use to guide your decision-making process (e.g., transparency, fairness, compassion).

☐ **Clarify Your Objectives:** What must the layoff process achieve (e.g., financial sustainability, preserving trust, honoring contributions)?

☐ Reflect on Past Experiences: Ask yourself:

- ❖ What have I learned from previous rounds of cuts?
- ❖ How can I do this differently?

Step 2: Plan & Prepare the Layoff Process

Purpose: Develop a clear, intentional strategy for how you will address the layoff process before any conversations begin.

Action Items:

☐ **Assess the Financial & Operational Needs:** Determine why layoffs are necessary and which positions are affected.

☐ **Explore Creative Alternatives and External Resources:** Identify possible internal transfers to other departments and your willingness to provide direct support through references and referrals.

☐ **Involve HR & Relevant Leaders:** Coordinate with HR to understand available resources, severance options, legal requirements, and expectations regarding roles and responsibilities.

☐ **Define the Timeline:** Plan key dates for notifying the entire team and individual employees, scheduling meetings, and conducting follow-up sessions.

☐ **Prepare a Communication Plan:** Draft clear talking points for communicating to both the entire team and individual staff directly impacted, that explain:

- ❖ The rationale behind the decision
- ❖ How the process was determined (fair, logical criteria)
- ❖ Next steps and available support

Step 3: Communicate Layoff Decisions with Clarity & Compassion

Purpose: Deliver the news to individuals directly impacted by layoffs in a manner that minimizes harm and builds trust, even in this difficult moment.

Action Items:

☐ **Schedule Private, One-on-One Meetings:** Choose a neutral space (or a secure video call) and plan for at least 30–45 minutes per conversation.

☐ **Deliver a Direct Message:** Use clear language, e.g., "Due to [reason], your position is being eliminated."

☐ **Acknowledge the Impact:** Validate the emotional weight of the news by saying something like, "I know this is incredibly hard."

☐ **Explain Next Steps:** Provide details about severance, benefits, and transition support. Provide a warm handoff to HR or other resource staff, if available.

☐ **Prepare for Emotional Reactions:** Remain calm and listen. Have a list of support resources ready (e.g., HR contacts, counseling options/employee assistance program information).

Step 4: Support Departing Employees Through the Transition

Purpose: Help employees leaving maintain their professional dignity and prepare for future opportunities.

Action Items:

☐ **Help Employees Frame Their Exit Story:** Provide neutral language they can use in interviews (e.g., *"Due to budget reductions..."*).

☐ Offer Tangible Support, if Warranted:

- ☐ Offer to be a professional reference and write LinkedIn recommendations.
- ☐ Connect individuals with hiring managers at other companies where they might be a good fit.

☐ **Connect Them to Resources:** Share contacts for networking, career counseling, résumé workshops, job placement, or external workforce development programs.

☐ **Coordinate with HR:** Ensure that exit meetings are handled with warmth, clear instructions, and empathy.

Step 5: Support Remaining Employees & Rebuild Trust

Purpose: Address cultural harm caused by layoffs, such as survivor's guilt and team morale.

Action Items:

☐ **Acknowledge the Loss:** Hold a team meeting to openly recognize the impact of the layoffs.

☐ **Share a Vision for the Future:** Clearly communicate new priorities and involve employees in shaping the next steps.

☐ **Provide Ongoing Support:** Offer one-on-one check-ins and create opportunities for team reflection and input.

☐ **Recognize Contributions:** Specifically, thank individuals for their efforts and ensure they know their work still matters.

Step 6: Practice Self-Care & Build Your Support System as a Leader

Purpose: Ensure that you, as the leader, maintain the capacity to lead with clarity, empathy, and resilience.

Action Items:

☐ **Set Boundaries:** Establish clear work-life boundaries and schedule time for self-care activities.

☐ **Seek Support:** Discuss challenges with mentors or peer support networks. Consider professional counseling or Employee Assistance Programs (EAPs).

☐ **Reflect Regularly:** Keep a leadership journal to process emotions, review decisions, and identify areas for growth.

☐ **Incorporate Mindfulness Practices:** Use short mindfulness or reflection exercises before and after difficult conversations.

Download the Full Checklist

Acknowledgements

This book would not exist without my partner, Shannon Lawrence. This project was her idea. And it was her unwavering belief that I should challenge my assumptions that pushed me to reflect more deeply on my experiences. Over the past two years, Shannon encouraged me to look beyond the logistics and numbers to the more human side of leadership in times of crisis. Through countless conversations, she urged me to interrogate my decisions, acknowledge my missteps, and find a way to articulate what I had learned. Her insight shaped not just the book, but the perspective I bring to this work. Beyond that, she meticulously combed through every word, lending her keen editorial eye to ensure clarity and precision.

I am also deeply grateful to my staff and faculty. Though we faced many real and difficult challenges, what stood out, again and again, was their deep care and commitment. They didn't just show up for each other; they showed up for the people they served. Their loyalty extended beyond our unit, reaching into every department and every student they supported. That level of dedication is rare, and I am grateful to have witnessed it firsthand.

To my Provost, thank you for your unwavering support throughout. I was never sure which of us had the harder job when it came time for layoffs, but I know you carried the weight of the entire division. You never dismissed the complexity of what we were navigating, and you understood that the leadership shift we were making wasn't just about budgets, it was about serving our people better. Your openness to change, your willingness to listen, and your steady leadership made all the difference.

This book is, in many ways, a reflection of the lessons I have learned from all of you. I carry those lessons with me, and I hope they will help others navigate the difficult, necessary work of leadership with the same care and conviction.

About the Author

Dr. Dan H. Lawrence is an educator, strategist, and lifelong learner with three decades of experience spanning libraries, nonprofits, higher education, and the public sector. His nonfiction centers on helping leaders navigate uncertainty with clarity, act with courage, and contribute meaningfully to the communities they serve.

With a background in educational leadership, instructional design, and information science, Dan brings a grounded and thoughtful approach to leadership and organizational change based in service. Through his writing, Dan invites others to pause, realign with their values, and lead with purpose even in the most challenging time.

www.ingramcontent.com/pod-product-compliance
Lightning Source LLC
Chambersburg PA
CBHW050442150626
46551CB00028B/1138